THE ESSENCE OF HOME

THE ESSENCE OF HOME

DESIGN SOLUTIONS FOR ASSISTED-LIVING HOUSING

by

William J. Brummett

VAN NOSTRAND REINHOLD
I(T)P® A Division of International Thomson Publishing Inc.

New York • Albany • Bonn • Boston • Detroit • London • Madrid • Melbourne
Mexico City • Paris • San Francisco • Singapore • Tokyo • Toronto

Cover Design: Paul Costello

Van Nostrand Reinhold Staff:
Editor: Jane Degenhardt
Production Editor: Carla M. Nessler
Production Manager: Mary McCartney
Interior Designer: Paul Costello
Interior Composition: Carla M. Nessler
Assistant Editor: Beth Harrison
Production Assistant: Carolyn Holfelder

Copyright © 1997 by Van Nostrand Reinhold

I(T)P® An International Thomson Publishing Company
The ITP logo is a registered trademark used herein under license

Printed in the United States of America

For more information, contact:

Van Nostrand Reinhold
115 Fifth Avenue
New York, NY 10003

Chapman & Hall GmbH
Pappelallee 3
69469 Weinheim
Germany

Chapman & Hall
2-6 Boundary Row
London
SE1 8HN
United Kingdom

International Thomson Publishing Asia
221 Henderson Road #05-10
Henderson Building
Singapore 0315

Thomas Nelson Australia
102 Dodds Street
South Melbourne, 3205
Victoria, Australia

International Thomson Publishing Japan
Hirakawacho Kyowa Building, 3F
2-2-1 Hirakawacho
Chiyoda-ku, 102 Tokyo
Japan

Nelson Canada
1120 Birchmount Road
Scarborough, Ontario
Canada M1K 5G4

International Thomson Editores
Seneca 53
Col. Polanco
11560 Mexico D.F. Mexico

All rights reserved. No part of this work covered by the copyright hereon may be reproduced or used in any form or by any means—graphic, electronic, or mechanical, including photocopying, recording, taping, or information storage and retrieval systems—without the written permission of the publisher.

1 2 3 4 5 6 7 8 9 10   EDW-AA   03 02 01 00 99 98 97 96

Library of Congress Cataloging-in-Publication Data

Brummett, William J.
   The essence of home: design solutions for assisted living housing/
William J. Brummett.
     p. cm.
   Includes bibliographical references and index.
   ISBN 0-442-02241-7
     1. Aged—Dwellings. 2. Congregate housing. 3. Architecture and the
physically handicapped.   I. Title.
NA7195.A4B78 1996   96-25480
725'.54—dc20   CIP

http://www.vnr.com
product discounts • free email newsletters
software demos • online resources

email: **info@vnr.com**
A service of I(T)P®

DEDICATION

To Tracey, Dolores, and Hulda

CONTENTS

Preface — *ix*
Introduction — *xi*

Part I: Understanding the Problem — 1

Chapter 1. **Defining Assisted Living** — **3**
Chapter 2. **Problem Discussion** — **25**

Part II: Paths Toward Solutions — 31

Chapter 3. **Conceptional Foundation for Design** — **33**
Chapter 4. **Architectural Design Considerations** — **39**
Chapter 5. **Behavioral Considerations** — **101**

Part III: Conclusions — 107

Chapter 6. **Illustrative Solutions and Conclusions** — **109**

Appendices

A. *Bibliography* — *133*
B. *Annotated Bibliography* — *139*
C. *References and Sources of Further Information* — *145*
D. *Approach and Method of Study* — *147*

Index — *153*

PREFACE

This book is about broadening and refining perspectives. It is about not being limited by outdated preconceptions; it is about reconceptualizing more appropriate, therapeutic, and enriching problem-solving approaches. Evolutions (and revolutions) begin in the mind. A simple questioning and rethinking of basic assumptions can lead to poetic invention and profound intervention.

This book is about architecture and its potential to meaningfully impact quality of life. Our actions, emotions, and thoughts are supported, directed, limited, and inspired by our perceptions of the natural and built environment. Our buildings are our memory and legacy.

Most importantly, this book is about improving the quality of the last years of lives of people whose aging has made them vulnerable and frail, and partially dependent on assistance from others to carry out the demands of daily life. Until fairly recently, this life-cycle phase was brief and these needs were met within a family structure and a supportive socioeconomic system. Today, this period of interdependence may span decades, and this supportive structure no longer exists.

Meeting the needs created by changes in our culture and medical practice, with solutions rich in therapeutic potential and meaningful choice, represents a fundamental challenge to today's society. Developing new and evolved approaches to solutions to this complex problem carries unique opportunity as well as social responsibility. A commitment to pursuing innovative, creative, and wholly responsive solutions can initiate a process that avoids the problems of overregulation, dependency, loss of personal freedoms, and exorbitant costs that have plagued much of the nursing home industry. Such a commitment can also yield great opportunity to define, direct, and shape a course of intervention supported by expanded and enlightened theories and methods regarding the most beneficial and enriching practices in housing and health care for the frail elderly.

This book began as a problem-seeking research project with the intent of clearly assessing the current definition and status of one new approach to a potential solution, Assisted Living, and illuminating issues needing further exploration. Responsive and supportive architectural design, particularly design which embraced homelike character, was one such domain requiring further study.

Supported by a National Fellowship for Research and Design of Healthcare Facilities granted by the American Institute of Architects and the American Hospital Association, and two Fellowships from the University of Wisconsin/Milwaukee School of Architecture and Urban Planning's Institute on Aging and Environment, exhaustive literature reviews, case studies of 24 innovative assisted living facilities nationwide, and interviews of 124 residents, staff, administrators, and family members were conducted.

It was found that although homelike character is considered a highly beneficial and desirable quality in an assisted living residence, it is rarely achieved by builders or designers, nor perceived by residents. Developing design direction for achieving homelike character naturally became the goal of the work.

A number of basic assumptions have been made herein—hypotheses that helped frame and direct the conceptual basis of this work. These include the beliefs that:

- *Architecture is an important component to creating the most therapeutic and enriching environs*
- *Homelike character is indeed an important and valuable goal*
- *It is possible to integrate this character in an assisted-living environment*
- *Comprehensive, conceptually founded study and analysis could illuminate paths toward reaching this goal*

Much has been substantiated by subsequent research, some is impossible to empirically or scientifically substantiate, and requires a calculated leap of faith.

This book is a modest step, an opening of dialogue about the impact and potential of the architectural component of the problem of appropriate housing and care for the frail elderly. It also represents a continuation of the discussion of the interplay between the image and phenomena of home and one's identity and well-being.

INTRODUCTION

Problem Context

America is aging. Advancements in medical practices and technology, as well as lifestyle changes, are enabling more and more people to live longer (Kane, 1990). When this factor is combined with the forthcoming population swell of the postwar baby boomers the significance of the aging of the population becomes apparent.

These same advancements in medical and other service fields are not only resulting in longer lives, but healthier and less-dependent lives. It is estimated that of this rapidly increasing population of 65+, only 20 percent will need long-term intensive medical care. The projected need for assistance with activities of daily living, however, accounts for over 68 percent of this population (U.S. Senate, 1991).

This dramatic rise in the elderly population, particularly the frail elderly, is fueling increasing concern for developing better solutions to their housing and health care problems. Both the public and private sectors are beginning to respond, as the government anticipates exponentially growing needs and the potential expense of meeting these needs, and developers monitor rising consumer demand. The U.S. Senate Subcommittee on Aging's Report (1991) recognized the significance of this trend:

"One of the most significant demographic facts affecting America's present and future course is the aging of its population . . . and the accommodation of their evolving special housing and health care needs."

Concurrent with this rapid growth in population is growing consumer dissatisfaction with current housing/health care options for elderly with special needs. The traditional custodial approach of care has received much criticism for its denial of patient individuality and its tendency to foster both physical and psychological dependence.

As holistic views on wellness and the factors which affect it become accepted, practitioners as well as patients and family members have begun to consider the quality and character of both care and the physical environment as significant contributors to one's health. This has lead to a widespread questioning of the environs typically created in traditional elderly housing/health care facilities (Kalymun, 1990).

New options for meeting the needs of this population, which generally requires intensive assistance (but not acute medical care), are developing to consider these issues. Assisted Living is one such developing solution that holds the promise of meeting these needs within a more acceptable and therapeutic environment.

Assisted Living represents a unique combination of services and environment. The definitive characteristics include a rich, assistance-intensive, individually and flexibly delivered service entity within a physical environment that embraces the qualities and character of *home*. The physical environment, in the Assisted Living model, is acknowledged as an active and supportive factor in the residents' wellbeing.

Problem Statement

The assertion that a "homelike" environment holds the most therapeutic potential for frail, semi-independent elderly has been a conclusion drawn recently and historically by a vast majority of leaders in the field of gerontology–environment studies (e.g., Regnier; Cohen and Weisman; Calkins; Hoglund; Kalymun). There is certainly little question of the emotional and psychological benefit of residing in a place more closely identified with the concept of "home" than one of "hospital" or "institution."

Of the 124 residents, family members, and staff interviewed in 24 assisted living facilities nationwide (Brummett, 1993), all but two volunteered the idea that a home or homelike environment was a primary goal, and was considered most desirable and beneficial.

Unfortunately, in the majority of emerging assisted living facilities, this goal remains unmet. Greater than three-fourths of the residents interviewed described their environment as something other than home or homelike. Many residents were found to refer to the (well-intended) decor and furnishings as "for the visitors" or "hotellike," indicating transience or lack of authenticity. Although homelike character is a highly desirable and valuable goal, it is not yet being widely attained by builders, nor felt by residents.

The solution to this problem of realizing homelike character and quality in Assisted Living is very simple: study *"home."* Look beyond its appearance toward its essence. *Home* is much more than a disconnected image. It is an interrelated set of spaces and of elements that together support many of our fundamental psychological needs as unique individuals living in a specific time and place and interacting with our community. Architectural critic Colin Rowe writes:

True freedom is not freedom from constraint, but freedom to be constrained only by what one truly is, by one's essence.

Attempting to recreate homelike character by simply applying a pastiche of exterior and interior decor (to what is, fundamentally, a hospital building) accounts for the perceived lack of authenticity, and unduly limits the possibilities of the most appropriate design responses.

This thesis suggests a realignment of the approach to designing assisted living residences. Rather than beginning with a nursing home or hospital model and attempting to camouflage it with decor, the forms, spaces, elements, qualities, and characters of home that truly support the essential concepts of home need to be considered. These can then be integrated with responses to the special needs of assisted living residents. This will be the process, task, and goal of this work.

Organization and Scope of Work

The organization of this work stems from the development of it as a graduate thesis—definition of terms, problem analysis, conceptual problem solution, and real problem solution. Chapter One will outline a clear definition of Assisted Living, both as a service entity and a work of architecture, within a system of elderly housing/health care service. Chapter Two will elaborate on the discussion of the problem and its components which began with the Problem Statement in the Introduction, and attempt to substantiate its extent, relevance, and constituent parts. A conceptual path toward solutions will be discussed in Chapter Three, which will be realized in Chapter Four as architectural design considerations, and in Chapter Five as outlined behavioral/service considerations that serve as additional context for architectural design. Chapter Six will discuss the design considerations and solutions as they relate to two case study assisted living projects, one theoretical and one built. Appendices provide literary and professional resources for further information.

The overall intent of this work is to illuminate paths and open channels that direct—not limit or prescribe—solution possibilities, solutions that hold the promise of profoundly realizing assisted living environments as home.

THE ESSENCE OF HOME

PART I

UNDERSTANDING THE PROBLEM

CHAPTER 1

DEFINING ASSISTED LIVING

DEFINITION

Assisted Living is a group-living arrangement for the physically and cognitively frail elderly where a wide range of individualized assistance is available 24 hours a day from a professional caregiving staff in a physical and operational environment that wholly embraces the quality and character of home.

Residents are typically considered semi-independent, often needing assistance with many activities of daily living, but are not long-term bedridden or in need of extended acute medical care. Caregiving staff deliver assistance as needed, with an emphasis on resident independence, autonomy, dignity, and shared responsibility. Residents are considered the primary decision makers with regard to their care and lifestyle. Their rooms are considered their private apartments within a supportive, extended family community.

NEEDS AND PROBLEMS THAT DRIVE ASSISTED LIVING

A meaningful understanding of Assisted Living begins with a clear knowledge of the needs and problems of the residents, for it is these concerns that underlie and direct the development and evolution of assisted living environments nationwide (Seip, 1989). Perhaps more importantly, it is these problems and needs that assisted living caregivers must address, family members struggle with and search for solutions to, and which precipitate a person's difficult decision to leave a long-time independent home and familiar lifestyle:

"Mom had her 87th birthday last week, and it broke my heart to see that she couldn't even gather enough strength to blow out

one candle. She's been living with us for two years now, ever since her stroke left her partially paralyzed and needing a wheelchair to get around. She was fine with us, here, up until the past few months. I'm afraid her physical, and sometimes mental, demands have gotten to be too great for our family to handle. She needs help getting into and out of bed, bathing, dressing, getting in her chair, grooming, toileting, and recently, she's had periods where she forgets where she is or how to get from one place in the house to another. She needs so much help, and I've gotten so afraid that she'll fall, leave the stove on, or have another stroke while I'm away at work that I call four or five times a day to check up on her. I can't concentrate on my work, and I need this job. We can't afford the 24-hour in-home nurse she really needs, and even if I could stay home to take care of her, I don't think I have the strength or expertise to really take care of her properly. But I can't put her in a nursing home. I saw my grandmother fade away, completely give up hope when she was put in a home. What am I going to do?"

—59-year-old daughter/caregiver

Thousands of elderly and their families face such difficult problems and situations daily. It is estimated that of the current population of 85+, 34.5 percent experience similar difficulties with activities of daily living (such as walking, dressing, transferring, bathing, toileting, eating), and 56.8 percent experience difficulties with activities of daily living and/or activities of independent household management (such as managing finances, preparing meals, completing household chores, shopping, getting around the community) (U.S. Senate, 1991). This at-risk or in-need population is projected to double in size by the year 2000, triple by 2030, and grow by a factor of seven by the year 2050 (U.S. Senate, 1991). (See Figure 1.1.) This partially dependent elderly population needs three times as many supportive services as those capable of living completely independently (Bernstein, 1982).

The specific abilities, disabilities, limitations, and needs of individuals within this frail elderly population vary, and may range from lower-assistance needs such as protective oversight to more intensive needs such as toileting or short-term hospice care. This variance in levels of assistance needed not only fluctuates from person to person, but through time, as a particular person's condition may change from day to day or month to month with short-term illness or infirmity, or as conditions develop or evolve (U.S. Senate, 1991; Brummett 1992).

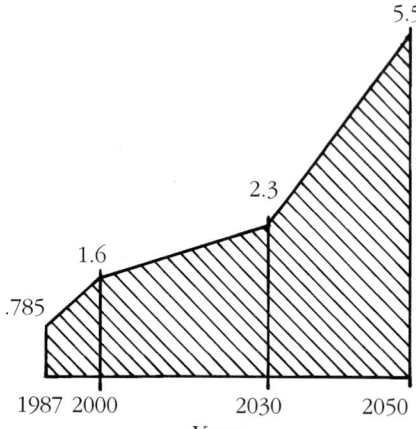

Figure 1-1 *85+ population with assistance needs, in millions.*

Assisted Living Residents' Common Problems and Needs

Residents' needs refer to both physical (functional) needs and those of emotional and psychological well-being. Often it is the physical needs that require the greatest amount of staff assistance, and can lead to higher levels of apparent risk. It is important to understand that unmet needs can often lead to untimely or unwanted discharge from an assisted living environment to a more intensive, institutional setting (AARP, 1993). The most "critical" categories of functional impairment are summarized below to highlight the importance of anticipating and responding to these needs:

Sensory Modalities

Residents who suffer from hearing, sight, speech, or tactile disabilities, or a limited ability to properly process the information they do receive may find particular difficulty in communication, orientation, and wayfinding. Degenerative cognitive impairments such as dementia or confusion and/or physical sensory impairments may limit a resident's ability to clearly comprehend a physical and behavioral environment and respond and interact in an appropriate manner (Calkins, 1988).

Mobility Impairments

Residents with difficulty walking or those who use wheelchairs, scooters, or walkers may find it difficult to travel long distances, access tight spaces, or reach a desired destination. Many may have difficulty accessing items in low, high, or deep spaces, or have difficulty with maneuvers or manipulations that may be necessary to perform activities of daily living. Although many residents can mobilize completely independently, moving about may be very slow, unsteady, cumbersome, strenuous, or even painful. Steps, grade changes, or difficult hardware may also present obstacles to independent access. For some, relatively immediate assistance and protective oversight in case of a fall or accident is a paramount need.

Incontinence

Some residents may have varying degrees of inability to control and self-manage bladder or bowel activity (Kalymun, 1990). This may be physiologically or cognitively rooted, and may be exaggerated by an inability to easily and quickly locate and access a restroom.

Security and Protective Oversight

Frailties, sensory impairments, mobility difficulties, and/or cognitive impairments may create situations or conditions (or the fear of such) that place a resident at a higher risk of accident or falling prey to criminal activity.

Meal Preparation and Monitoring

Many residents, because of fatigue, inability to access markets, or inability to properly plan and prepare complete and nutritious meals, may need meals prepared. Those with cognitive impairments may require cueing to remind them to take meals.

Medication Monitoring and Assistance

Most residents require multiple medications with special (and often complex) administering regimes. If these regimes are not properly followed, potentially dangerous effects could result (AARP, 1993). As a result of confusion, dementia, or sensory or dexterity impairments, some residents may need assistance, monitoring, and/or cueing to properly take their medication.

Grooming and Hygiene Cueing and Assistance

Some residents may be physically or cognitively unable to consistently and appropriately bathe, toilet, groom, or dress themselves without assistance or cueing.

Ability Maintenance and Enhancement

Appropriate physical, intellectual, and emotional support, stimulation, and challenge are important needs addressing residents' well-being and sustenance of quality of life.

Respect of and Opportunities for Expression of Choice, Control, Dignity, Privacy, and Independence

Respect for these issues is a profound and fundamental need and right for residents' emotional and spiritual well-being, and acknowledges residents as whole, capable, and adult individuals.

Connections to Normalcy—People, Places, Activities, and Things

The transitions in activities, environments, and lifestyle that can occur with a person's decreasing abilities very often represent a loss of familiarity and sense of rootedness, orientation, and belonging. Opportunities for connections to people, places, things, and activities that are normal (i.e., normally experienced in their home setting), familiar, and beloved can potentially soften the transition and lessen the loss (Fewster, 1989).

Figure 1.2 illustrates the relative likelihood of a resident needing assistance with particular activities of daily living (U.S. Senate, 1991).

Persons with needs and conditions that generally extend beyond the abilities or scope of assisted living environments include persons who are long-term or permanently bedridden; persons who consistently require intravenous medication or other daily acute medical attention by a physician; persons in a comatose or other vegetative state or otherwise completely unable to communicate their needs; or

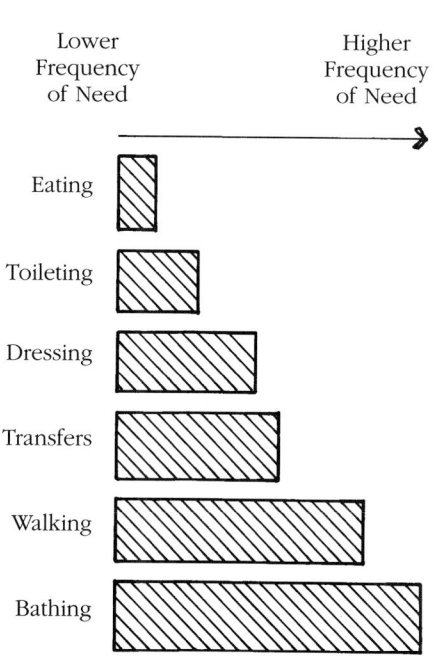

Figure 1-2 *Frequency of assistance needs.*

those with dementia or other degenerative cognitive conditions of an advanced state. It should be recognized that many assisted living facilities allow residents to contract outside (of facility operation) in-home health care or hospice care to deliver more intensive services on a relatively short-term basis, where permitted by law.

Resident Profiles

The following profiles have been drawn as a means of describing the depth, breadth, and variety of needs and problems of typical assisted living residents (Brummett, 1992 and 1993; Wilson, 1990; Regnier, 1991):

Lower Intensity-of-Assistance Needs

Profile 1: A person of good physical and mental health who lives alone and, because of general frailties and slight sensory impairments, feels vulnerable to accidents and/or crime and thus seeks the security of group living and professional protective oversight. This person may also be less able to travel to social places and functions and, hence, may seek the camaraderie and companionship of group living.

Profile 2: A person of fair health but with chronic physical frailty. The burdens of household chores such as cooking and cleaning may be too strenuous, difficult, or consuming for this person. He or she may also seek protective oversight.

Profile 3: A person who is in good physical health but suffers from relatively consistent (yet relatively slight) confusion and disorientation. This person may seek protective oversight, professionally delivered meals, medication and cleaning services, and occasional behavioral cueing and assistance.

Profile 4: A person with a combination of the above physical and cognitive needs.

It is important to realize that while the less intensive of these profiles may be appropriate for "elderly apartments" or other group/peer living arrangements, which provide meal, laundry, housekeeping, and social services but no assistance, an anticipation of the potential for future and significant assistance needs with advancing age, and a preference to limit the number of relocations (Brummett, 1993), very often prompts the decision to enter an assisted living residence.

Higher Intensity-of-Assistance Needs

Profile 5: A person who maintains most cognitive skills but has developed more-intensive physical frailties and disabilities. These may include limiting (as opposed to debilitating) mobility impairments requiring dependence on a wheelchair, scooter, or walker and some transfer assistance; severely decreased strength and coordination of his or her hands or arms requiring assistance with many activities of daily living; respiratory ailments causing shortness of breath and inability to perform many activities; sensory impairments causing some communication and orientation difficulty; and/or incontinence and a limited ability to self-manage this.

Profile 6: A person who maintains most physical abilities but has a decreased cognitive ability, often the result of Alzheimer's disease or other organic brain dysfunctions. This person may have relatively regular or extended periods of moderate disorientation to time and place, and may require consistent and redundant behavioral cueing and assistance in order to appropriately carry out activities of daily living and any needed therapy. This person may also have a few brief episodes of disruptive behavior necessitating intervention.

Profile 7: A person with a combination of the above physical and cognitive disabilities requiring regular and intensive assistance.

These profiles are intended to describe the wide range of needs, abilities, and dependency/independency levels of assisted-living residents. This underlines the importance of flexibility and adaptability of the physical and operational environment. The ideal is to anticipate this range of needs and consider each resident's needs as unique and dynamic, affording for individual/local accommodation and change, as opposed to projecting the most intensive of these need levels and hence designing the service delivery and environment to the lowest common denominator.

Traditional Responses to These Needs

In order to distinguish Assisted Living from other forms of elderly housing/health care, introduce the reasons for its evolution, and place Assisted Living within the continuum of elderly housing/health care services, it is useful to describe this continuum and the traditional options for addressing the needs discussed. (See Figure 1.3 for a typical continuum model.) This continuum and the options which attempt to meet the needs will be discussed in terms of three key characteristics: 1) services and service level provided; 2) ability to embrace a normal, homelike environment; and 3) relative cost. (See Figure 1.4.)

Traditional Option One: Shared Household with Loved One/Caregiver

The most traditional method of meeting the needs of this frail elderly population is to share a household with a family member or friend who is capable of providing the needed assistance and oversight.

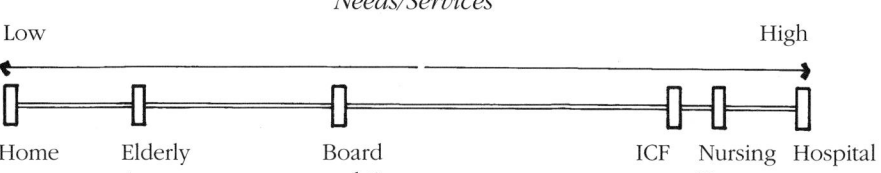

Figure 1-3 *Traditional continuum of care model.*

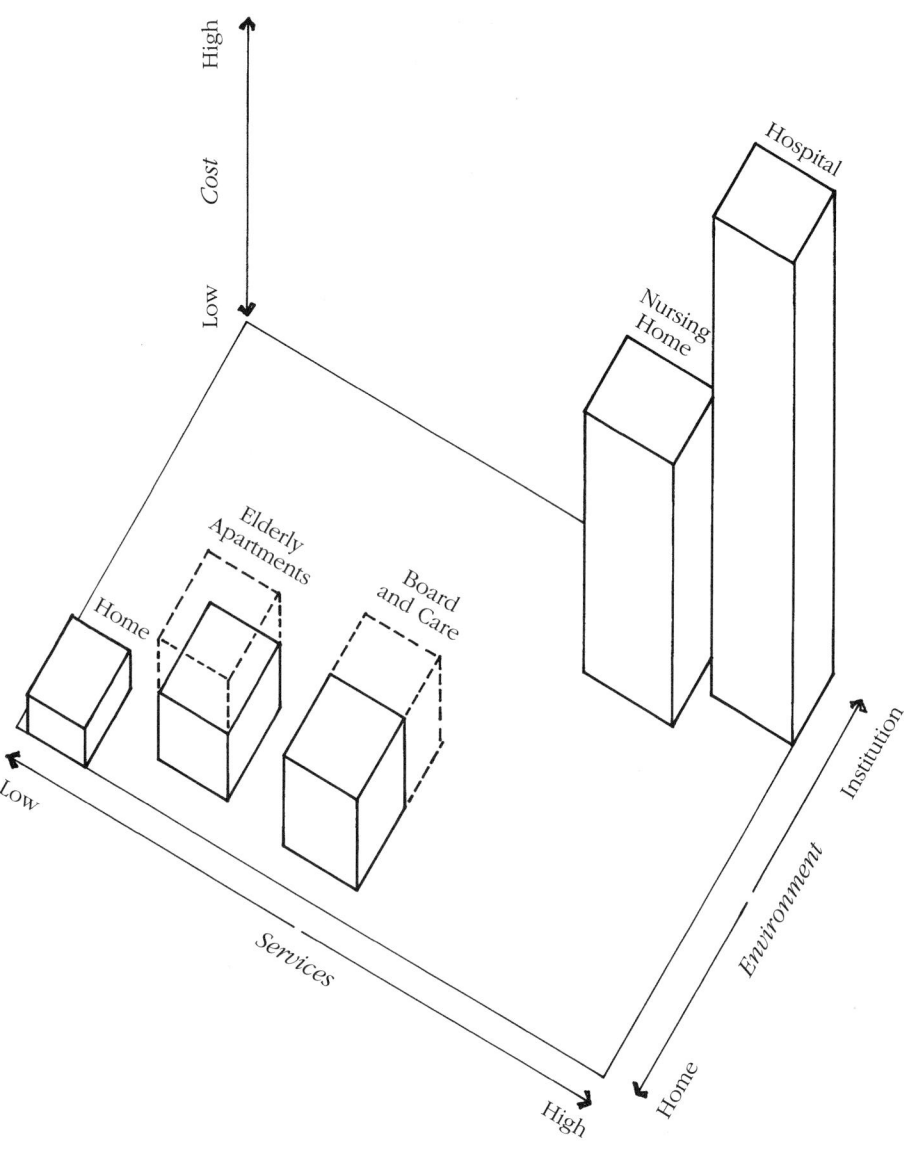

Figure 1-4 *Multidimensional continuum of care model.*

Indeed, until the last 50 years, this was the only option in this country other than nontherapeutic institutionalization (AARP, 1993). While at lower levels of care, this option may be quite viable. However, such a responsibility can represent a significant change in lifestyle and opportunities for the caregiver.

Services

The character of the service delivery is often born of love and care, and the arrangement itself renders an entirely individualized and catered "system" of service delivery. Typically, however, the level of sophistication of care available is limited by the level of expertise, training, and experience of the person providing the care. Also, the availability of additional assistance for the caregiver (i.e., to aid in transfers, etc.) as needed is typically nonexistent or requires careful scheduling. As the need for assisted transfers increases, the actual physical limitations of the caregiver may be reached.

In many cases, the physical limitations of a house not adapted for handicap accessibility may impede access to some areas of a household to one with mobility impairments and other physical frailties.

Because of these limitations, as well as the physical and emotional stress that can often be induced by such an arrangement, this option is often most appropriate for shorter durations.

Homelike Character

Of course, since the physical environment is in fact not only literally a house, but usually a known and comfortable home, the character of the environment is optimal.

Relative Cost

The initial direct costs of this shared household arrangement is relatively minimal when compared to the cost of other elderly housing/health care options. Prior to the development of state and federal assistance for such, this was often the only economically reasonable solution for many.

This option, however, is fostered by a socioeconomic climate that enables one head of household to be available to provide the needed assistance and oversight. As this climate has evolved into one necessitating two incomes, the viability and effectiveness of this arrangement has faded.

Traditional Option Two: Professional In-Home Health Service

Another potential option for receiving care in an independent home is contracting professionally delivered in-home health services. Because this method allows a person to remain in his or her own home and typically offers a very high level of service, it is the most preferred option (Brummett 1992 and 1993).

Services

Services are typically highly individualized and specialized regarding the particular needs of the resident, and catered to the resident's preferred schedules and routines. In addition, the caregiver is usually a registered or licensed professional trained in assistance/caregiving and emergency care. With prudent caregiver selection, service in this option is at its utmost level of quality and consistency.

Homelike Character
This method of service delivery causes the least amount of disruption in one's life by affording one to remain in his or her own home, in their community and among familiar things and places. Connections to routines and expected events remain intact. Additionally, the relationship between caregiver and recipient is most likely to become established as one in which the care receiver is empowered, as the caregiver is a guest in the care receiver's home.

Relative Cost
Unfortunately, while this housing/health care option is most desirable concerning many issues, its cost is typically so high that it eliminates this as a reasonable or possible alternative. For short durations, or at a moderate part-time schedule, this option may be viable for some. But for extended periods of time and/or for 24-hour live-in care, this option is typically only affordable to those of significant financial resources.

Traditional Option Three: Board and Care Homes

Board and care homes are traditionally smaller "mom and pop" operations or smaller facilities run by charitable organizations that usually house 1–3 nonrelated frail or cognitively impaired persons in a house with a live-in caregiver/owner/operator (Kalymun, 1992).

Services
Service is typically delivered by the live-in owner (or manager) and 1 or 2 part-time assistants. Twenty-four-hour protective oversight, meals, laundry, housekeeping, and some assistance with activities of daily living are usually provided (AARP, 1993). In most jurisdictions, operators of board-and-care homes are required to be specially trained and professionally licensed and/or registered, ensuring an appropriate level of competent care.

Since the acceptance of mobility-impaired, incontinent, or transfer-dependent residents, and the administration of medications, are generally prohibited and beyond the reasonable scope or expertise of many board and care operations (AARP, 1993), this option does not fully respond to many of those most in need. In addition, as discussed in Traditional Option One, a house may have many physical barriers to handicap accessibility.

Homelike Character
Most board and care homes are operated from within an existing home or small-scaled, residential building, and their setting is often within an existing residential neighborhood fabric. Additionally, since

this option of care is delivered within a small, familylike setting, familiar home environment and relationships often develop and are nurtured (Kalymun, 1993). Typically these factors combine to foster a genuine homelike setting.

Relative Cost

Of key issue regarding the cost of board and care compared with other options is its acceptance/rejection by governing agencies as being eligible for state and/or federal assistance for its tenants. Although the board and care industry is beginning to experience its own evolution, to date many agencies are a bit cautious regarding the level of consistent professional care administered, and hence do not provide financial assistance for its tenants. Thus, although the actual cost of board and care is substantially lower than nursing homes, the relative out-of-pocket expense to the tenant (and the tenant's family) is often higher (AARP, 1993). Many families are forced to choose a nursing home environment over a board-and-care simply because of board-and-care's lack of government subsidy.

Traditional Option Four: Nursing Home

For the purposes of this work, intermediate care facilities, rest homes, skilled nursing facilities, and nursing homes are all considered under this category. Although the level of care given within these does vary, the environments and philosophical approach to service delivery are very similar.

Services

Nursing homes provide extensive services including meals, laundry, housekeeping, assistance with activities of daily living, transfer assistance, medication monitoring, security and protective oversight, and many other social and medical services short of intensive procedures and monitoring by a physician. Until the emergence of Assisted Living, in most cases this was the only option for those with moderate assistance needs, impaired mobility, confusion, or inability to self-manage incontinence (Hendrickson, 1988).

Even within a fully developed continuum of care community (one which affords all options of elderly housing and health care) nursing homes may indeed represent the most appropriate service environment for those with long-term intensive needs.

The service model/approach of nursing homes (in part mandated by extensive government regulation) is one that places all decision-making control and responsibilities with staff, and is highly routined and uniform. This tends to dismiss residents' needs to maintain any sense of autonomy, dignity, control, or choice. Residents live within a world where they are powerless to control even the care of their own body. Aside from the potential psychological and physical effects of this situation, the uniformity of care delivery can often lead to those with less intensive needs being overserviced, which may result in an accelerated degenerative status (Regnier, 1991).

Homelike Character

The physical environment of a nursing home is hospital-like, being traditionally designed and regulated after the medical model. Such an environment is very well suited to efficient, effective, and economic service delivery and maintenance. Unfortunately, the psychological effects of this environment on its residents, who must attempt to make a home in this atmosphere, are ill-considered. Long, double-loaded corridors with sterile, shiny floors, grid ceilings with fluorescent tube fixtures, televisions mounted on steel shelves at the ceiling, and a visually dominating nurse command station hardly create a warm and comfortable home environment. The sense of alienation, hopelessness, and loss of identity and individualism is usually (and understandably) immense and devastating.

Relative Cost

The cost of providing services under this model represents a tremendous burden on both consumers and governments (U.S. Senate, 1991). Overservicing, and a physical and operational environment that fosters dependence and lethargy combine to create a truly wasteful and ineffective system. While government assistance and subsidy encourage nursing homes as an option over many other elderly housing/health care alternatives by reducing the out-of-pocket cost to residents, society as a whole must pay for this antiquated approach through higher taxes and an overtsressed Medicare system.

THE EVOLUTION OF ASSISTED LIVING

A number of key factors have led to the need and consumer demand for assisted living. Advances in medical knowledge and practice are enabling people to live significantly longer and healthier lives (Kane, 1990). People living well into their 90s and 100s is becoming more and more commonplace in the United States. The number of people aged 100+ is expected to increase by 40 percent between the years 1989 and 2000 (U.S. Senate, 1991). Many who reach their upper 80s and older are relatively healthy, needing some assistance but not intense care. Unfortunately, this exponentially increasing demand for housing options for this population of elderly needing longer-term assistance but not acute medical care is not being appropriately met (U.S. Senate, 1991; Kalymun, 1989).

The evolution of medical and environment-behavior research, practice, and theory—has lead to an acknowledgment and support of the therapeutic potential of the physical environment:

> *"Ecological theories underlying a continuum of care framework include Lawton and Nahemow's (1973) Competence and Environmental Press Theory and Kahanas's (1975) Congruence Model of Person Environment Interaction. Both*

these theories maintain that interactions between older individuals and their environment produce outcome behaviors. These persons are influenced by levels of functional competence, or needs and preferences and the demand characteristics of the physical environment. The extent to which interactions between elderly people and the environment complement one another determines positive or negative outcome behaviors. The more vulnerable elderly people are, the more likely it is that their behaviors will be affected by the environment."

—Kalymun, 1990

In particular, noninstitutional and homelike environments have been heralded as carrying greater therapeutic potential for this population (Cohen and Weisman, 1991; Calkins, 1988; Pastalan, 1992; Wilson, 1990; Kalymun, 1992; Kane, 1990; Regnier and Pynoos, 1994).

The rising cost and financial burden of nursing care has prompted the search for supportive yet less expensive alternatives for meeting the needs of this population. Recent studies (AARP, 1993; Kane, 1990) reveal assisted living facilities can be as much as 40 percent less expensive than nursing homes serving people with similar needs.

These factors have lead to an increasing consumer awareness, concern, and demand for new housing options that provide the needed intensive service level within a homelike environment and at lower cost.

Assisted Living developed as a response to these issues, locating itself in the broad and significant gap that existed between board and care facilities and nursing homes. (See Figure 1.5.) Initially evolving in the late 1970s and early 1980s as a more sophisticated board-and-care-like environment (Kalymun, 1992), Assisted Living aims at maintaining similar homelike qualities, character, and individualized services, while expanding the service and social/activity options, maturing the service delivery system, providing accessibility to the mobility-impaired, incontinent, and confused, and taking advantage of reasonable economies of scale.

Studies of European elderly housing/health care approaches, philosophies, and accommodations (Hoglund, 1985; Regnier, 1994 and 1992) have provided fresh inspiration and models of progressive and innovative solutions that are expanding and enriching the assisted living paradigm.

Conceptual Definition of Assisted Living

There are two key components of the better models of Assisted Living. First is that of a service-rich, comprehensive, flexible, and individually assessed and delivered assistance and care provider. Crucial to this component is the ability for residents to choose those services they require from a range of methods in which these services are delivered, representing a continuum of service delivery from independency to dependency. Also implicit in this notion is an approach to delivering

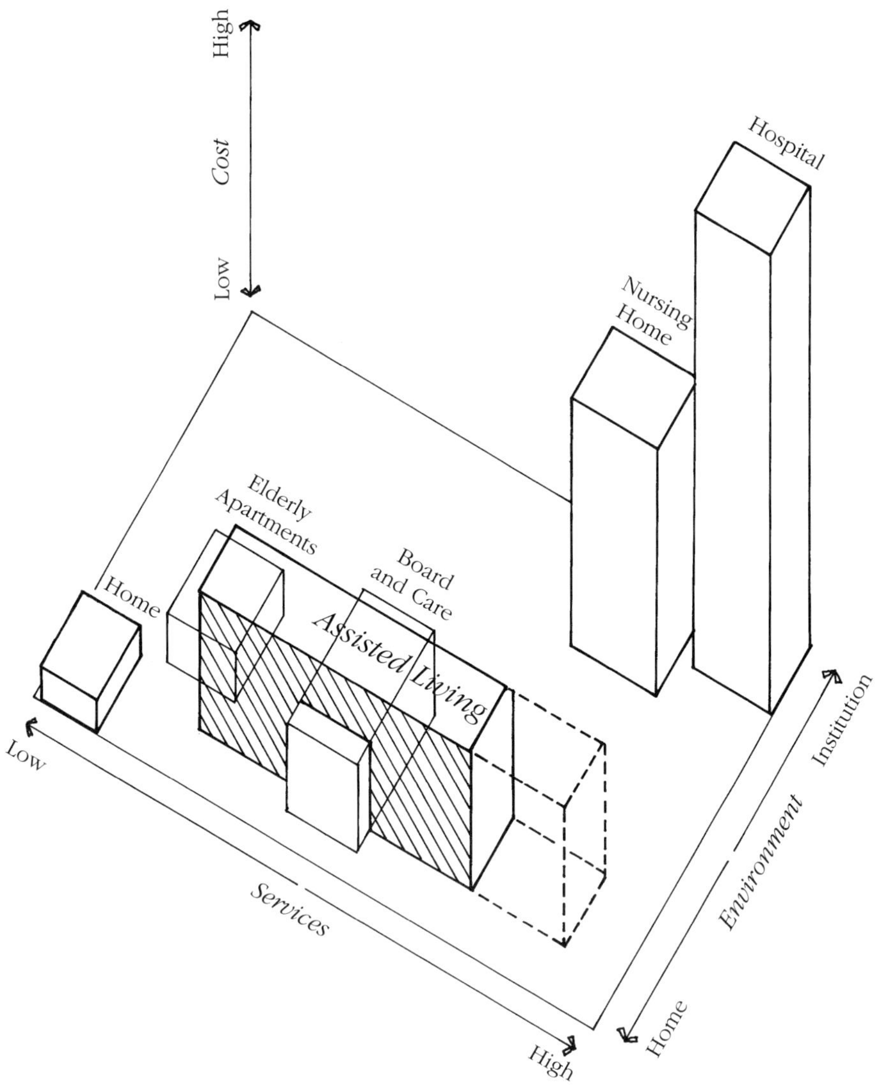

Figure 1-5 *Multidimensional continuum of care model with Assisted Living.*

services to residents on a case-by-case basis that is periodically evaluated and adjusted to meet changing needs. This evaluation is a partnership, between resident, family, and staff, whose common goal is maintaining the abilities, dignity, and autonomy of the resident.

The second component of Assisted Living is that these services are offered within a physical and operational environment that provide as much of the normalcy, autonomy, comfort, and stimulation as experienced at home. Not only should the environment present a physical and spatial experience throughout that is homelike, it should also provide and afford the same opportunities for normal, homelike and communitylike social interaction and activities of daily living as experienced at home.

ASSISTED LIVING AS A SOCIAL PHENOMENA

Assisted Living indeed represents a significant paradigmatic shift in more-intensive, larger-scale for-profit elderly housing and health care. Assisted Living illustrates the changing attitudes about the potential quality of life and care for the frail elderly, including their abilities, rights, and potential contributions.

Philosophy and Principles of Assisted Living

The following principles (adapted from Wilson, 1990) are fundamental to the better models of Assisted Living:

1) ***Choice/Control/Autonomy:*** The ability to make choices and decisions, and develop and consider options that carry responsibility and influence meaningful outcomes. This also implies having control over one's own private space and the activities and therapies one undertakes.

2) ***Privacy:*** The ability to reach a place of retreat or seclusion and be free of unwanted intrusion. This applies to both a place and private behavior or activity, including the ability to receive treatment without intrusion by, or the knowledge of, others.

3) ***Dignity:*** The acknowledgment and respect of one as an individual with abilities, freedoms, and rights as extended to all people, and as capable of enrichment of both self and others.

4) ***Independence:*** The affordance of opportunities to contribute to, and carry out, tasks of one's own maintenance of well-being. The ability to perform meaningful, useful, and enjoyable tasks and activities and make worthwhile decisions as an individual and valued person. The ability to act as a unique person, including identifying with, and personalizing of, one's own space.

5) ***Familiarity and Attachment with One's Environment:*** The ability to understand, identify, and occupy the imageful, spatial, and material qualities of the place as a familiar comfortable home.

6) ***Safety/Security:*** The ability to live in the comfort of a controllable and responsive environment, reasonably free of undue or unaccepted risk or hazard.

7) ***Accessibility:*** The accommodation of all spaces, elements, and routes for easy access for those with mobility, sensory, and cognitive impairments.

8) ***Adaptability:*** One's ability to reasonably adjust the activities, therapies, behaviors, and physical environment to respond to one's changing needs, desires, and competencies.

9) ***Stimulation/Challenge:*** The opportunity to yield physical, intellectual, and emotional reward from one's activities and environment while maintaining safe and acceptable levels of risk.

Services Offered in Assisted Living

Most residents do not necessarily require all services; some residents may require some at more intensive or dependent levels and other residents at more independent levels. Service needs are dynamic and may develop temporarily or over time. The ability for residents to choose desired services, the level of need, and manner of delivery is definitive to Assisted Living. Monitoring and evaluation of service needs is considered a shared responsibility among the resident, the resident's family, and the caregiving staff.

1) ***Personal Care:*** Grooming, bathing, dressing, eating, ambulation, transfer, toileting, laundry, and housekeeping.

2) ***Medical Assistance:*** Monitoring of medication; intervention of conditions before a physician is needed; counseling; appointment-making; supervision. Additional assistance or medical services in-residence, contracted through in-home healthcare or hospice care, may be an allowable option at very intensive need levels.

3) ***Security and Protective Oversight:*** Twenty-four-hour emergency call and medical alert, as well as the security of being in a group environment with alert staff and friends.

4) ***Meal Preparation:*** At least two prepared meals a day if desired, often with some flexibility with regard to entree selection and scheduling of meals.

5) ***Social Activities and Community Connections:*** Enjoyable and therapeutic opportunities for social exchanges within facility and community; professionally directed exercise; accessibility to religious activities; occasional planned excursions.

6) ***Commercial Connections:*** Many facilities offer some sort of store where groceries and personal items can be bought; a place to get a haircut, shave, and/or manicure; cafe or other place to get an informal meal in a normalized social setting.

7) ***Transportation:*** Some mode of chauffeured transportation accessible to those who are frail or mobility impaired.

Assisted Living as a Building Type

The purpose of this section is to provide an overview of the general and preferred aspects of the physical environment of assisted living facilities in order to set a basic context for further elaboration. Detailed descriptions, analyses, recommendations, and design considerations will be discussed in Chapter Four.

Context

Assisted living facilities are typically situated in semiurban (dense housing and commercial mix), suburban, or small community settings. Freestanding facilities represent 51 percent of existing assisted-living facilities (Seip, 1989). Location of an assisted living level within a Continuing Care Retirement Community (CCRC) campus is another typical application. Many residents and family prefer stand-alone models because of their representation of stay longevity (i.e., residents not being convinced to "move up the ladder" to higher levels of care in a CCRC campus). The smaller size of a stand-alone facility may also foster more direct and meaningful staff-resident interactions, and better integrate within the surrounding community.

The benefits of belonging to a larger CCRC campus often include more in-house social services, commodities, and opportunities, and the security of nearby higher levels of care within the campus.

Architectural Program

Spaces provided in an assisted living facility usually include some larger, more active spaces for group gatherings and events, as well as smaller, more intimate shared spaces; dining room and service kitchen; a number of small assistance spaces, such as a bathing room and a medicine storage location; a few smaller staff work spaces; and a reception/oversight area. Between 12 and 130 resident apartments are usually provided. Typically, 25–60 units are most preferred and viable (Seip, 1989). Additional social and service spaces, such as a small market or store, library, activity kitchen, beauty parlor, food service entity, or chapel, may be provided, depending on the size of the facility and availability of such services nearby in the community. (See Figure 1.6 for a typical architectural program.)

Building Organization

Although a relatively central staff reception/monitoring point is important for safe and efficient operation, its location is neither mandated nor regulated by law, therefore it does not drive the scheme of the assisted living residence design with the same influence as it does in nursing home design. Also, the intention to minimize the impact of the staff monitoring space suggests that this element not dominate design.

Typical overall building organizations range from a central entry with wings (see Figures 1.7 and 1.8), an exterior or interior courtyard or cloister (see Figure 1.9), or a clustering of units (see Figure 1.10). Single-loaded corridor arrangements are highly preferred to double-loaded arrangements.

Building Character

Attempts to embrace and integrate the character of "home" throughout the design include issues of building massing, image, scale, purpose and nature of rooms; arrangement and sequencing/layering of rooms; interior and exterior finish materials; details and textures; lighting; and furnishings. These issues and strategies for appropriately addressing them will be discussed at length in Chapter Four.

ARCHITECTURAL PROGRAM
CORVALLIS ASSISTED LIVING

Space	Sq. Ft.	Equipment	Notes
SHARED SPACES			
Dining Room	650	China cabinet	Small tables seating 4–8
Living Room	460	Fireplace	Accommodate larger group activity
Family Room	240		Informal gatherings
Library	160	Built-in bookshelves	Quiet, smaller groups
Activity Kitchen	140	Sink, refrigerator, lockable stove and oven, dishwasher, casework	Connection to dining
Lobby/Vestibule	140–240	Wanderguard exit system	Connection to reception, mail, and main circulation
Mail	80	40 6" x 6" lockable mailboxes	
Resident Laundry	100	2 washers, 2 dryers, adjustable ironing board, folding table	
Restrooms	2/floor @ 60	Frail handicap accessible	Connection to dining
Storage	1200		
Porch			8' deep
Total	3,810		
STAFF SPACES			
Kitchen	550	Commercial dishwasher, oven(s), stove, refrigerator, freezer, sink(s), shelves, countertop, casework	Direct connection to dining
Kitchen Storage	200	Shelves	Direct connection to kitchen
Reception/Observation	160	Alert systems, phone, work surface, lockable casework	Unobtrusive yet relatively central
Office	140	Alert systems, phone	Connection to reception
Staff Retreat	150+	Refrigerator, sink, casework, countertop, microwave	Private: includes restroom and private outdoor space
Assisted Bathing	140	Alert systems, accessible whirlpool bath	
Staff Laundry	140	2 washers, 2 dryers, folding table, ironing board	
Med/Prep	60	Lockable casework, countertop sink	
Total	1,590		
RESIDENT APARTMENTS			
(25) Studios	Each 320		With closeable, separable sleeping area
(12) 1–Bedroom	Each 480		
(3) 2–Bedroom	Each 600	* ALL APARTMENTS to have own frail-accessible bathroom with sink and shower; kitchenette with sink; lockable stove and oven; small refrigerator; accessible casework and countertop; built-in display case(s); and alert systems in bathroom and sleeping areas	
COFFEE HOUSE/BOOKSTORE			
Coffee House/Bookstore	600	Bookshelves, tables for 2–4 people	Connection to park
Prep	350	2 sinks, commercial dishwasher, warming oven, refrigerator, freezer, 2 espresso machines, mixer, display cases	
Storage	180	Freezer	
Restrooms	2 @ 60		H.C. accessible
Total	1,250		
Mechanical	600		
Circulation	5,305	(25% total building—single-loaded corridor)	
Total Building	**27,275**		

Figure 1-6 *An architectural program for an assisted living facility for 30 residents. (From Corvallis Assisted Living, William Brummett, Architect.)*

Figure 1-7 *Plan showing a scheme with central entry and two wings. (Rosewood Estates, Roseville, Minnesota. Reproduced with permission of BRW Elness, Assoc.)*

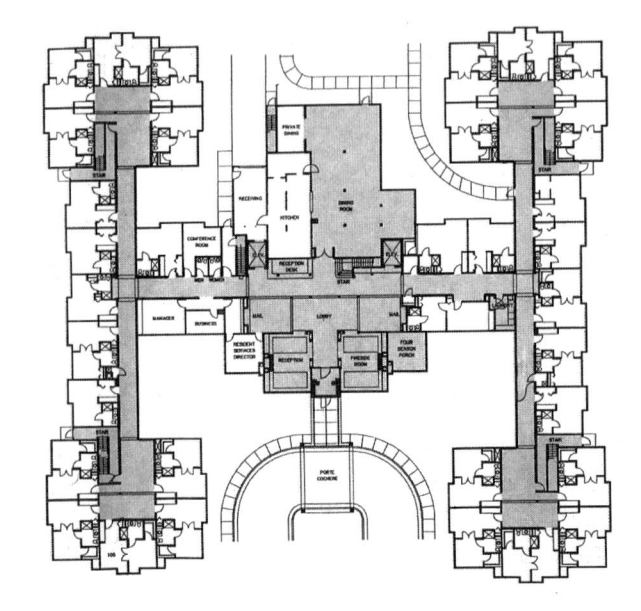

Figure 1-8 *Plan showing a scheme with two single-loaded wings. (Annie Maxim House, Rochester, Massachusetts. Reproduced with permission of Barry Korobkin, Architect.)*

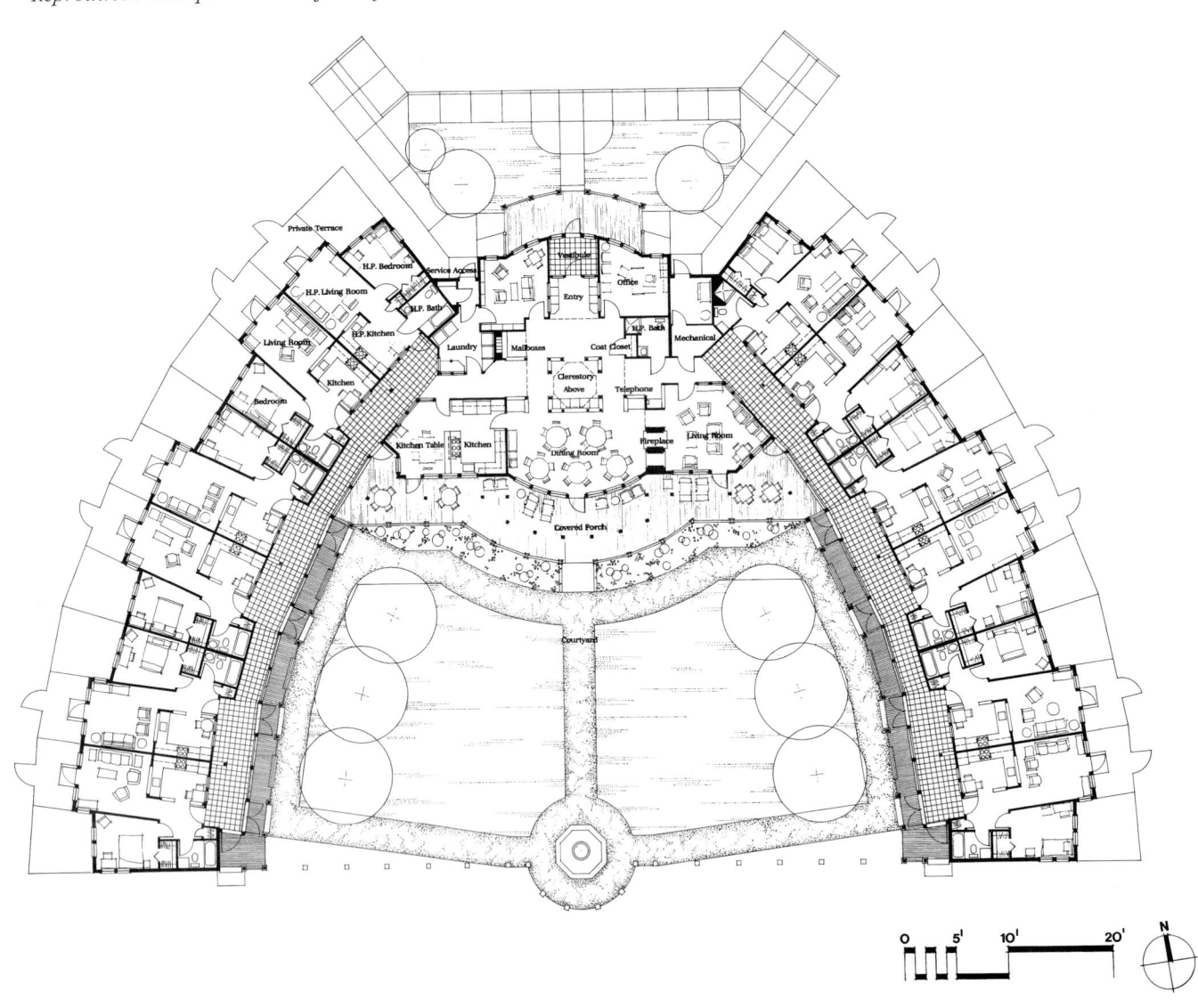

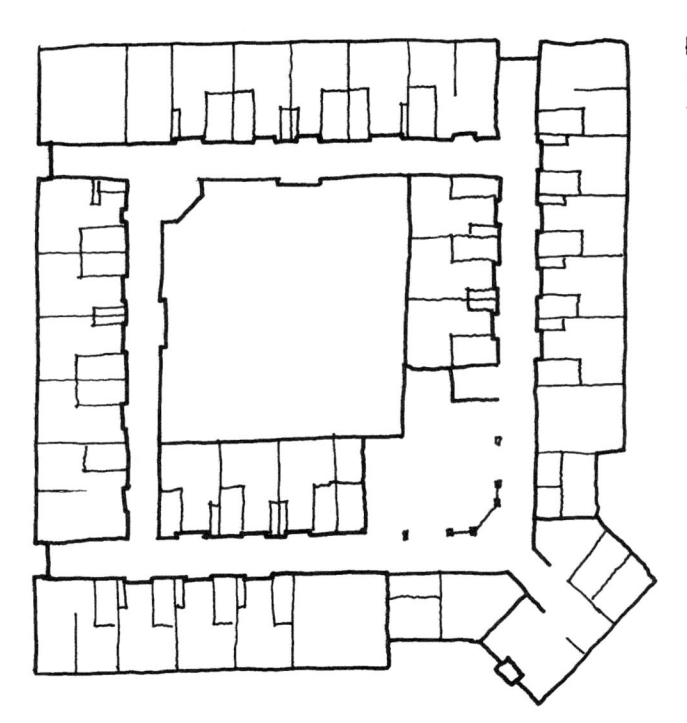

Figure 1-9 *Plan showing a courtyard scheme. (Rackleff House, Canby, Oregon. Reproduced with permission of Chilless-Nielsen Architects.)*

Figure 1-10 *Plan showing a scheme with a series of clustered apartments. (Woodside Place, Oakmont, Pennsylvania. Reproduced with permission of Perkins Eastman Architects.)*

Woodside Place

1. Entry
2. Administration
3. Great Room
4. Main Kitchen
5. Library
6. Sitting Area
7. Country Kitchen
8. Living Room/Dining Room
9. Pantry
10. Single Bedroom
11. Double Bedroom
12. Quiet Room
13. Music Room
14. Arts & Crafts Room
15. Entertainment Room
16. Secure Courtyard
17. Secure Wandering Area
18. Patio
19. Service Yard

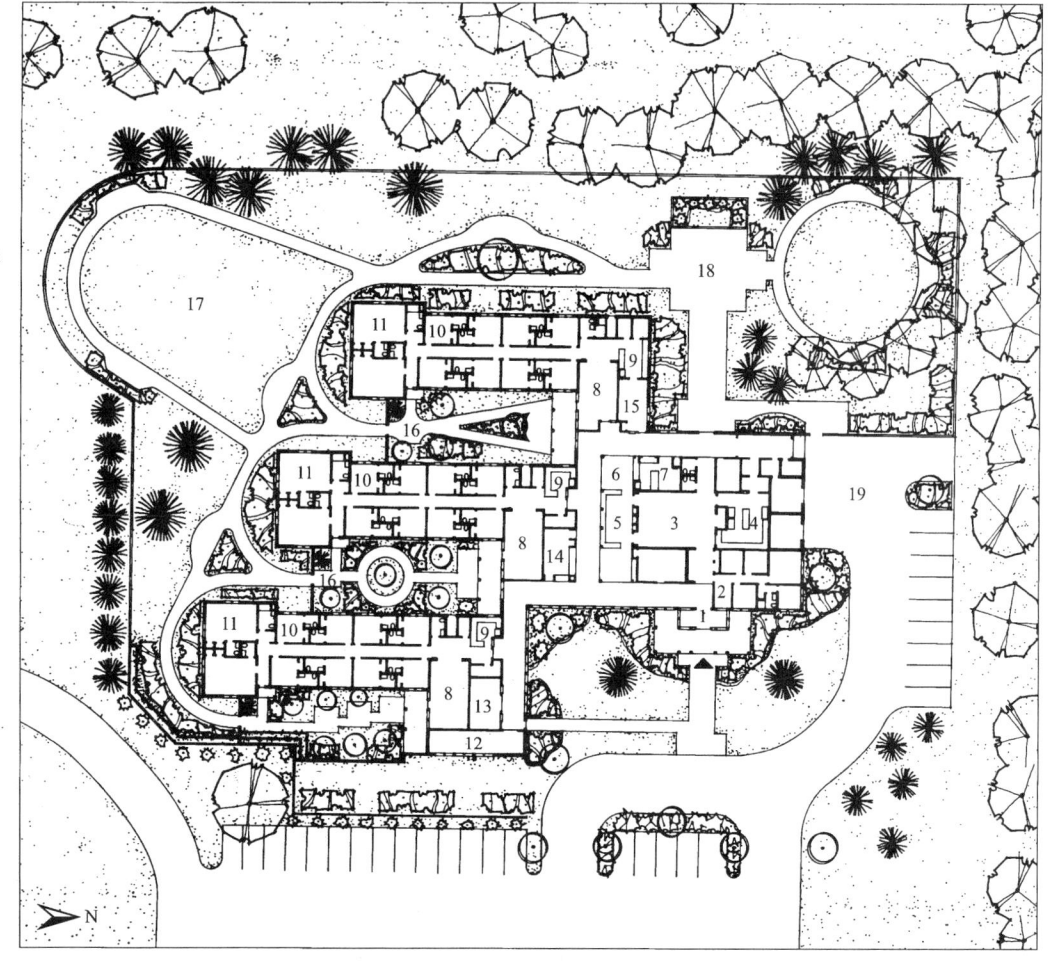

DEFINING ASSISTED LIVING

Resident Apartments

Fully equipped single-occupancy resident apartments are the architectural cornerstone of Assisted Living (Kane, 1990). A private apartment (unless chosen otherwise by a resident, as in the case of a couple sharing an apartment) is indeed the only arrangement that truly supports the fundamental notions of privacy and autonomy that are definitive to Assisted Living.

Apartment plans vary greatly (see Figure 1.11) and, in fact, most facilities offer a variety of apartment plans for residents to choose. Private baths with accessible fixtures and roll-in showers; kitchenettes with a sink, stove/oven (often removable or switchable), and refrigerator; lockable doors; and individual Heating, Ventilation, and Air-Conditioning (HVAC) controls are provided. The better apartment plans are designed to shelter or screen the bedroom or sleeping area from direct view from apartment entry. The better models include some private outdoor space, balcony, or deck. Accessibility to maneuver a walker or wheelchair within all features of the room, or ease of adaptability for such access, is paramount.

Regulation

Because of the relatively embryonic state of Assisted Living, regulations vary greatly from state to state and are in an equally developing and somewhat ambiguous state. Areas of regulatory concern fall into three general categories:

1) The licensure of Assisted Living as a professional assistance- and service-providing entity.

2) Potential qualification for state and/or federal funding and reimbursement.

3) Building codes.

A complete state-by-state description of current and likely regulatory requirements is far beyond the scope or intent of this work. (See AAHA 1992 in the Bibliography for a workbook/handbook to state codes reference.) Following is a general discussion of the issues concerning regulation.

Licensure requirements for assisted living residences and staff are often modified versions of board-and-care regulations (Wilson, 1990). These primarily focus on the functional status of residents, the intensity of the services required, and the physical environmental features of the facility (Kalymun, 1992). These often impact the type, extent, and delivery systems of the services provided, and the physical spaces, equipment, and communication/emergency systems required.

As this book is going to press, Oregon's Medicaid Waiver Act was the only organized system for state and federal subsidies to assist those of lower incomes accessing assisted living care (with the excep-

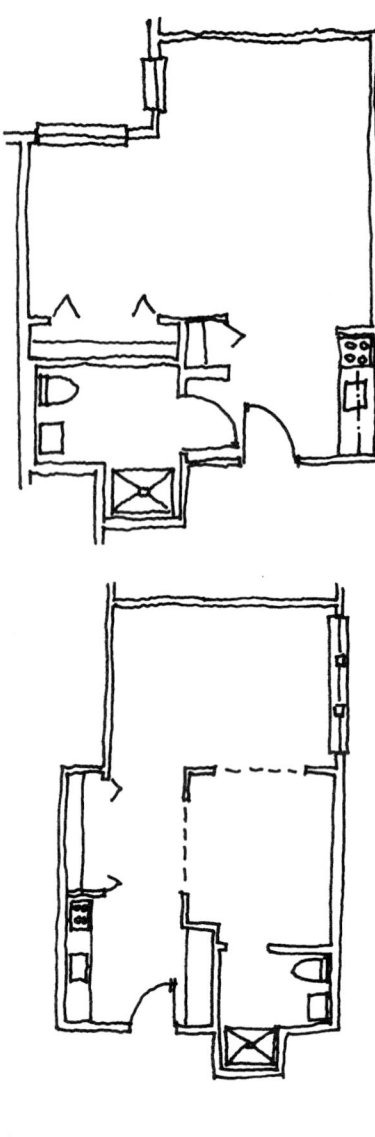

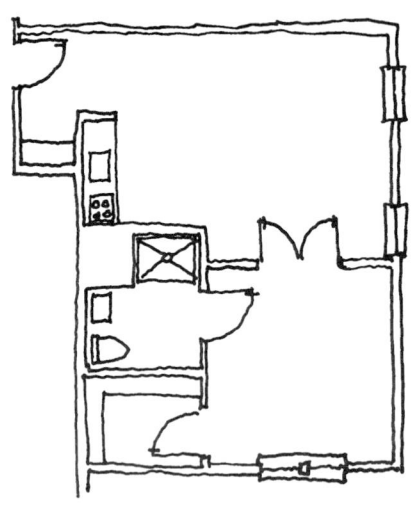

Figure 1-11 *Three apartment plan variations showing different levels of accessibility, privacy, and cost. (Rosewood Estates, Roseville, Minnesota. Reproduced with permission of BRW Elness, Assoc.)*

tion of a scattering of a few small pilot projects). However, both state and federal governments are beginning to investigate the potential implications, therapeutic benefits, and savings of doing so.

Building code requirements depend primarily on the interpretation of Assisted Living as an "I" institutional or "R" residential occupancy group, or the development of an occupancy group or subgroup specifically addressing Assisted Living. This interpretation may vary not only from jurisdiction to jurisdiction, but often from building official to building official. Key issues, such as required fire protection, corridor widths, material and equipment specification, and required spaces, often drive up the construction cost and threaten to undermine the homelike character of the facility if interpreted rigidly or conservatively. Increased education and awareness about this new building type, as well as the development of new safety and emergency systems and finish materials, hold promise for an acceptable reconciliation of safety and normalcy.

Because of the complexity and current dynamic nature of Assisted Living regulation and its varied local interpretation, it is highly recommended that the services of a professional regulation/code analyst be enlisted as an invaluable member of a building design's project team.

Practical Advantages of Assisted Living

Lower Cost

As stated previously, Assisted Living offers a level of service equitable to nursing homes (for those not requiring intensive medical care) at a savings of up to 40 percent. This is due in large part to the more effective and efficient service delivery approach which attempts to reach the most appropriate ratios of staff to residents without compromising care.

Assisted Living's evolving enlightened regulatory system is beginning to foster this decrease in operating costs by limiting bureaucracy and mandates which promote inefficient and ineffective dependence-supporting service. In addition, the establishment of more appropriate building codes, guided by contemporary architectural practices, help reduce the construction cost, which in turn reduces life cycle costs and the cost of financing.

These factors become amplified by the fact that up to 35 percent of residents currently in nursing homes could be more appropriately housed and cared for in assisted living residences (U.S. Senate, 1991).

Appropriate Regulation

As a newly evolved and developing housing and health care service system and building type, comprehensive nationwide regulation of assisted living facilities is not yet in place. This unique situation affords the system's leaders rare opportunity to carefully conceive and orchestrate its regulation. Freed from the paradigms and regulatory foundations of the past, which lead to the prototypes for nursing homes and other institutional care, Assisted Living's development and regulatory foundation can be informed by research and knowledge directed by the most appropriate and progressive therapeutic ideals.

New notions of individual and flexible service delivery, independence fostering, and the important effect and influence of the physical environment can be integrated into the conception of its regulation. Great savings of both time and money by government regulatory agencies, practitioners, and residents are becoming evident and anticipated.

Economies of Scale

Assisted Living strikes a balance of number of residents, between the complexity and potential alienation of larger facilities, and the inefficiencies of many of the smaller board-and-care homes. With a preferred number of residents between 25 and 60, an assisted living residence is large enough to achieve the most effective staff-to-resident ratios without compromising service quality or effectiveness, yet small enough to be administered relatively simply and with an appropriate degree of flexibility.

More-Productive Members of Society

Perhaps the most profound practical advantage of the entire approach and philosophy of Assisted Living is its potential to increase the activity, productivity, and richness of a community of people. The fundamental notions of fostering assisted-living residents' abilities, independence, and individual values encourages continued participation and engagement in community events and processes. Residents are thus more likely to regard themselves as assets to their community family, as opposed to liabilities. Such engagement not only expands a community's richness and potential, but supports and strengthens the acknowledgment of the continued value of people as they age.

CHAPTER 2

PROBLEM DISCUSSION

INTRODUCTION

The search for the best models of Assisted Living naturally branches into two realms of research, development, design, and implementation:

1) Initiating the most responsive and therapeutic assistance/service delivery systems.

2) Embracing the most profoundly homelike environments.

These avenues mirror the two fundamental characteristics that define Assisted Living.

While the service-delivery questions continue to evolve and develop, the majority of the solutions to the problem of truly creating home environments have stalled, falling short of their promise to reach levels of maturation, sophistication, and synthesis.

Certainly, this problem has both behavioral (staff and resident relationships and attitudes) and architectural roots. It can be argued, however, that the architecture sets the tone of the environment and thus cues behavior in a manner which is most salient and subtle, and yet difficult to change.

This trend is recognized, at an academic level, by the current and continued notation in research and literature that homelike character is a problem not yet comprehensively resolved. More importantly, it is acknowledged by the fact that the vast majority of assisted living facilities' residents do not inhabit and embrace their environment as "home" (Brummett, 1993).

The current trend in the architectural design of Assisted Living attempts to attain homelike character primarily through the employment of exterior and interior finish materials which are similar in appearance to those one would find in a typical house. This approach is the logical initial offspring of the advancing theories (as well as marketing prospectuses) of appropriate assisted living environs. It represents a beginning to the evolution of the architectural design of Assisted Living, for it is the first physical (and economic) manifestation of the recognition that the most desired, beneficial, and therapeutic environment for the frail elderly is home.

Indeed, to many visitors and passersby, these environs initially appear homelike. Yet this approach has not yielded its desired response. These environs may appear as home, but they do not instill residents with the belief or understanding that they *are* home. They do not embody or bring to life the essence of home.

Impact and Relevance

If the place where one resides is not a *home*, then what is it? One is left searching for clues that fix a place and cue attitudes and behaviors. It is possible to imagine a place primarily identified with illness and declining health to cue dependency and loss of hope; a place primarily identified with transcience to cue lack of engagement and retreat; and a place with unclear, little, or contradictory identities to cue disorientation.

These ideas of the character and identity of place affecting behavior and psychological (as well as physical) wellness rely on two bodies of theory and research:

1) the relationship between the physical environment and behaviors and attitudes; and

2) the notion that "home" is uniquely critical to support wellness.

Research discussed in Chapter One illustrates and substantiates current theory relating the physical environment to behavior. The environment not only limits and directs our movement and occupation of a place, but the character of the environment shapes our perception of the appropriate and expected behaviors, attitudes, and moods about it. The character of the environment conveys (intentionally or not) the meaning of the place and the nature of our interaction with it.

Current trends to "soften" or "humanize" hospital, prison, and other institutional environments reflect the acknowledgement that the physical environment plays an important role in affecting the psyche and, hence, behavior and wellness.

The connections between one's sense of identity and wellness and the concepts and realizations of the phenomenon *home* have been the subject of discussion from philosopher Martin Heidegger

Building Dwelling Thinking to architect and sociologist Clare Cooper-Marcus *(House as a Symbol of Self)*. In these works home is identified as the reflection or first concrete permanent object substantiating one's identity and sense of place and purpose within a larger group. The inner haven of the home is a private and safe sanctuary; it is the vessel holding the icons that place memory in space and time. The outer shell of the home is the image one desires others to have of oneself. Thus, "home" is the primary and fundamental environment that concretizes and symbolizes our security, sense of self, consistency, and orientation in the world. Without home, one of our primary mechanisms which symbolizes how, where, and who we are is absent. The loss of home represents a tremendous, irreplacable loss and profound threat to well-being.

Constituent Parts of the Problem

The problem of creating homelike character in Assisted Living has two dimensions:

1) How does one create or embrace the character of home? (i.e., what is the character of home?)

and

2) How can this be integrated in an assisted-living environment?

The Question of Homelike Character

The problem inherent in the first question (what is the character of home) lies in the depth of understanding. The question is how to understand "home" in a way that enables us to create assisted-living environments that do not just *look* like home, but *work* like home, and support the activities and conceptual notions that truly make a place a home. This requires an analysis and discussion of the concepts, ideas, and principles that underlie the physical manifestations of "home."

If the intention is to reach a richer and more meaningful image of home, then the critical questions which can direct design are:

1) What are the more broad, universal, and relatively eternal concepts of home that can be generalized and put to use?

2) How does home architecture support, nourish, and bring to life these concepts in a meaningful and lasting way?

Exploring the first question represents the fundamental step necessary to reach the most satisfying and compelling solutions. The second question compels one to consider architecture at a more comprehensive level. Rather than simply considering the visual questions of home architecture, it is necessary to consider the spatial, sequential, and elemental dimensions as well.

This kind of analysis and understanding is what is needed to move beyond the stylistic interpretations and facade treatments to create assisted living environments that capture the architectural essence of home. This kind of understanding holds the potential to give designers of assisted living environments new tools and new freedoms. Chapter Three will begin this type of analysis of home in an attempt to open and broaden this channel of discussion, and to reconsider what design decisions will move us in the direction of embracing homelike character, in a more lasting and meaningful way.

The Question of Integration

Understanding the second dimension of the problem (e.g., How can homelike character be integrated in assisted living residences?) begins by recognizing the obstacles to the integration. The obstacle to integrating the concepts and services of *Assisted Living* with *home* is that inherent in the definition and purpose of Assisted Living are potential contradictions to "home." These contradictions can be described as follows:

Potential Contradictions

1) ***Resident needs and responses to those needs*** in the form of behavior and environment may stretch beyond the traditional, conceptual, or "normal" realm of "home." Appropriate response to resident needs is fundamental to the philosophy of Assisted Living. The distinction that is important here is that assistance and care are not necessarily synonymous with a dependent relationship between resident and caregiver. If these needs are addressed in a manner that consistently places the resident in a primarily dependent role, then a contradiction is developed between "home" and "a place where care is given."

2) ***Living in a group situation*** could compromise some of the principles of home through intrusion on one's privacy and territoriality. Economic and pragmatic efficiencies and realities limit the housing options of those with intense support/assistance needs to group settings. Living in a group situation places new stresses on the concepts and principles of "home" including privacy, territoriality, control, familiarity, and individuality. Questions of the clear identification of a place as one's own, appropriate behaviors of admittance/retreat, and personal identity in one's own space within a larger group whole, are of paramount concern.

    Issues of the identity of, and appropriate behavior for, each shared space among a group of many individuals also becomes important.

    However, living in a setting with others of generally similar experience also offers new opportunities for connectedness and belonging.

3) ***The introduction of caregiving staff*** and their needs and procedures could conflict with behaviors and environments associat-

ed with the notions of home. Even with an emotionally supportive, respectful relationship between staff and residents, staff members still must assume responsibilities and tasks that could dilute the realization of "a place like home" with "a place like work" and "a place where care is given." Such is the case in a typical nursing home, where the physical and operational environments are designed to support the staff and their work almost exclusively, irrespective of the fact that residents live there.

4) *Higher levels of standards regarding safety and well-being* of residents could suggest behaviors and architectural realizations that conflict with homelike behaviors, procedures, and environments.

Standards and regulations with respect to procedures and construction often imply institutional behaviors, routines, and environments, which in turn undermine many of the concepts of home.

The interpretation of the health and safety of residents to reside only within considerations of physical well-being, requiring hospitallike solutions in terms of environment and procedure, is the conceptual relic that is at the root of this problem and must be discarded.

This discussion of the two dimensions of the problem of creating homelike character in assisted living environments begins to reveal both the complexity of the problem and nature of the work toward the solution. The solution to the problem is not seen as an appliqué of "home style," but instead as involving both architecture and procedure/behavior, requiring a richer understanding of "home."

The second section of this book will attempt to synthesize conceptually founded architectural issues of home with strategies for mitigating these potential contradictions.

PART II
PATHS TOWARD SOLUTIONS

CHAPTER 3

CONCEPTUAL FOUNDATION FOR DESIGN

INTRODUCTION

The discussion of the concepts of *home* begins by defining the term *concepts of home,* and describing its limits and context. The ideas for discussion herein, which will form the foundation for deriving architectural design considerations, are a range of concepts which could arguably be considered relatively general, universal, and eternal—those which do not significantly change over time or space, nor are significantly affected by individual personality or experience. Some may question the notion of such universal concepts, arguing that individual cultural, historical, and personal experience colors one's formation of, and identification with, such concepts. However, many have proposed that there are fundamental concepts which transcend far beyond individual experience (such as Carl Jung, in his formation of the notion of universal and eternal archetypes), focusing on the fundamental condition of a meaningful human experience on earth.

The limits of applying such broad-based concepts are misinterpretations of the realization of the concept (the building), particularly over a wide cultural or historical gap. Although the general population of assisted living residents is not necessarily culturally and historically homogeneous, it is asserted that these differences of experience within this group are not of a depth nor magnitude to render significantly different understandings of, and responses to, such fundamental concepts. This limitation does call to the forefront, however, the importance of integrating design responses to conceptual notions with local interpretation and context.

The context for the concepts of "home" refers to the "setting" in which they are embodied, realized, as well as evaluated (consciously or subconsciously.) This context involves action as well as physical settings. A simplified model suggests the concepts of "home" are embodied and realized in an interaction of activities of daily living, social activities, the physical environment, and the psyche, in a relationship where the physical environment acts as a supportive and interactive stagelike vessel, and all is interpreted according to the state of the psyche. (See Figure 3.1.)

The importance of understanding this context is twofold. First, it clearly illuminates the interactive quality of the concepts and the importance of addressing home as an environment of behavior and activity as well as architecture. This interactive context for the concepts of "home" suggests the importance of the inclusion of Chapter Five, "Behavioral Considerations," in this book, even though the primary focus herein is on the physical environment. Secondly, it illuminates the importance of considering the concepts of "home" as an initial step in the design process, and employing them as a gauge and meter to architectural as well as procedural design. If a primary goal of Assisted Living is creating a homelike environment, then using the concepts of "home" as a prime evaluating and developing tool most profoundly ensures a result most consistent with, and authentic to, the notion "home."

In this context, the notion of concepts of "home" is derived from a line of thought regarding what "home" represents, or symbolizes. Clare Cooper-Marcus (1974) writes:

"Man selects the house, that basic protector of his internal environment, to represent or symbolize what is tantalizingly unrepresentable. As we become accustomed to, and lay claim to, this little niche in the world, we project something of ourselves into its physical fabric."

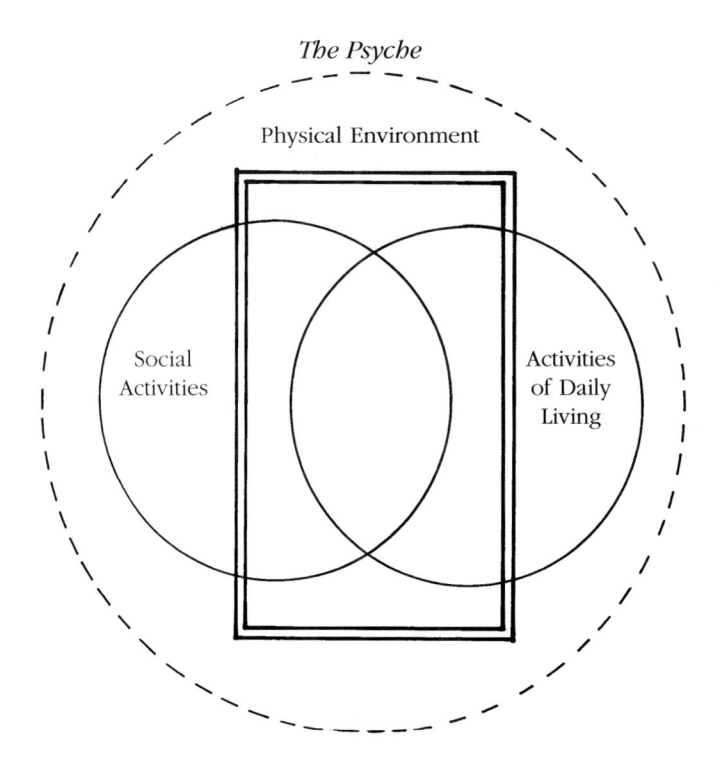

Figure 3.1 *Home Concept Interpretation Diagram.*

Philosopher Martin Heidegger puts forth an even more aggressive claim, suggesting that, particularly in "house," man builds with intention (consciously or subconsciously). In building and dwelling within "house," man seeks to establish not only his image of self, but of the world and his relationship to it.

Speaking of the house as embodying our understanding of the world in which we live, Norwegian poet Tarjei Vesass writes:

"The house stands there, singing . . . The house sings about how the inhabitant has managed to come to terms with his environment. It radiates what he has obtained from being in the world."

Architect Christian Norberg-Schultz, in his treatise "The Concept of Dwelling," continues the discussion of the meaning and symbolism of home and its concretization of our relationship to the greater world around us. The house is a physical and psychological fixed point in a relatively unknown and changing world:

"In the house, our wandering has come to an end. The house brings the inhabited landscape close to man, and thus it becomes the cradle from where we can start our wandering again."

This body of work begins to illuminate the meanings and symbolism of "home," its conceptual foundation. Throughout these and similar essays, two veins of thought occur and reoccur. These can be categorized by two realms, or groupings, of modes of being: Home as a symbol of self—**identification,** and home as a symbol of one's relationship to the world—**orientation.** A third category, house as a symbol of one's condition—**qualification,** can be drawn which overlaps each of the other two categories, yet has distinctions of its own.

Simply put, we have to know who we are, how we are, and where we are to experience life as meaningful. Home is the manifestation of our attempts to come to grips with our sense of identification, orientation, and qualification.

The question may be asked "Does a typical contemporary home really carry with it so much symbolism?" The answer is, of course, yes (for example, see Scott-Brown, 1977). It is just that this process of instilling meaning is veiled by its familiarity. The building of a contemporary house is typically based on accepted patterns of settlement, design, economics, and construction. This symbolism is embedded in these patterns over centuries of evolution. The process thus becomes an almost subconscious act of very slight modification of a theme or solution set that is wrought with meaning.

The problem concerning Assisted Living is that group elderly housing has been typically based on a hospital model or building type, rather than a housing typology. This pattern has developed over time, and is ingrained in our way of thinking about this building type. As our notions of appropriate care and physical environments have evolved, it is necessary to make a conscious effort toward realigning elderly housing design with the notion which we now understand is so important to it—home.

The Concepts

Within each mode of being, identification, orientation, and qualification, a number of individual concepts emerge that speak of the essence of home in relation to this mode. These form the foundation of the social, organizational, and environmental norms that describe a setting as home. These concepts are presented in pairs of consistent, yet slightly divergent notions in order to suggest their inexact nature.

Identification

The concepts within this mode both reflect and project who we are, who we have been, and who we may become.

Self-Projection/Self-Symbol

Home is a place where one can express one's identity as a unique individual, and one's status as an important part of the community. Home has both an interior, sacred realm, reflecting how one sees (or wants to see) oneself, and an exterior outward facade, reflecting how one wants to be viewed or regarded by others.

Vessel of Memory/Vessel of Soul

Home is a place where one finds the things one covets, finds important, meaningful, beautiful, or useful. It is a place of continuity, where the things that hold memories or symbols of our personal family history are kept.

Home is a place where one enters the world, learns of the world, and prefers to die.

Connectedness/Belonging

Home is a place where one gives and receives love and support as a member of a family. It is where one feels worthy, of value, and an important contributor to greater whole, a place where one understands one's being part of the world. It is a place offering opportunities for meaningful connections with peers, one's community, and other communities.

Orientation

Concepts within this mode speak of where we are in relationship to both known, fixed points and the unknown; how the environment, at a small and large scale, is organized and occupied.

Center/Origin

Home is a fixed and stable center, from which to embark into the greater world, and which to return to from the unknown; a sacred realm in the profane world.

Familiarity/Order

Home is a place where one feels comfortable, uninhibited, and relaxed. It is a known and restful place where destinations, relationships, and organizations are understood and are reasonably adaptable to one's changing needs and desires.

Stability/Predictability

Home is a place where reasonable expectations are met and anxieties alleviated, a fixed place where properties and relationships are known and change only when desired.

Privacy/Territoriality

Home is a place that accommodates times of solitude, quiet reflection, rest, and intimacy without unwanted intrusion. It enables one to set clear boundaries that describe norms for attitude, admittance or retreat.

Qualification

This mode of being groups together concepts that speak of the condition of one's existence.

Security/Safety

Home is a place of shelter from threats and the elements, a place where one can perform, act, and rest in safety.

Control/Autonomy

Home is a place where one has reasonable control over the characteristics of the environment and the behaviors that happen in it. It is a place that allows and supports one's freedoms and rights as a capable person.

Choice/Opportunity

Home is a place where one chooses one's own lifestyle, image, and activity, a place that supports a variety of desired activities and one's ability to select one's place among them. It is a place that provides opportunities for engagement, excitement, and interaction; a place of possibilities for challenge and stimulation.

These concepts:

- *Self-Projection/Self-Symbol*
- *Vessel of Memory/Vessel of Soul*
- *Connectedness/Belonging*
- *Center/Origin*
- *Familiarity/Order*
- *Stability/Predictability*
- *Privacy/Territorxiality*
- *Security/Safety*
- *Control/Autonomy*
- *Choice/Opportunity*

together form the time, space, and experience-transcending symbolic content of "home." When considered as design generators, and when tempered with response to the individual design problem and context, they represent a profound key to directing the creation of assisted living environments rich in the qualities and characteristics which speak of the essence of *home*.

CHAPTER 4

ARCHITECTURAL DESIGN CONSIDERATIONS

Introduction

Context and Use

To this point, the conclusions drawn have been Assisted Living-specific, but somewhat general in architectural terms; they have been intended to set a conceptual framework. The following design considerations are meant to be more architecturally specific, although not in a manner that is limiting or prescriptive, but in a manner that illuminates the issues and usefully illustrates approaches to solutions in relatively concrete, architectural terms. The hope is that these will inspire responsive and creative solutions.

Although the design considerations are intended to consider a variety of contexts of Assisted Living design problems, it should be noted that a particular given situation could render some of the issues more directly appropriate, meaningful, and applicable than others. Such issues include specific physical building context; scope and scale of facility; level of integration of the cognitively impaired subpopulation of residents; and management and operational philosophy, as well as the designer's values, interpretive system, and creative will. These issues should weigh, edit, and direct the interpretation of these design considerations, as well as inspire the development of additional design issues.

Derivation of the Design Considerations

This chapter represents a distillation of a process of study. The concepts of "home" discussed in Chapter Three have been used as a springboard and measure for studying the meaning and relevance behind home architecture. Common threads of architecture and accommodation were found which, although not necessarily realized through identical design response, do speak of recurring issues, themes, and characteristics. These characteristics have innumerable combinations and articulations, but together begin to form a basis for design which creates the environment *home.*

These architectural characteristics of home were then integrated with Assisted Living-specific issues to arrive at sets of architectural design considerations which are intended to direct design and to illuminate the relevance and importance of addressing such issues.

The goal of this chapter is not to address all of the design issues of Assisted Living (since many design issues are site and program specific, such a task is impossible), but rather to discuss the issues most salient with regard to creating homelike characteristics in an assisted living environment.

Structure of the Architectural Design Considerations

Since the architectural design considerations are derived from the concepts of home as put forth in Chapter Three, they are organized according to their relationship to each concept. This results in an atypical sequence of architectural issues (a common ordering of architectural design issues would likely move from large-scale to small-scale issues, such as site issues, overall building issues, detailed building issues, etc.). However, this organization most intimately describes the connection between the concepts and their derived architectural issues, and on careful study, seemed most appropriate and clear.

A number of the concepts are supported by architectural characteristics and resultant architectural design considerations which, admittedly, overlap one another. Although this results in a certain degree of reiteration, it clearly demonstrates the interwoven and imbricated nature of the concepts and their manifestations, and it illustrates the potential for these manifestations to yield a richness of meaning.

The images chosen to illustrate various points were selected for their ability to do so, as well as to describe the widest possibility of context and style. An important image selection criteria as well was to offer architectural design particularly rich in quality and character. These criteria were not limited by an image selection group of only Assisted Living facilities, as is evident. The intention to enrich readers' "image bank," by offering a selection of the finest works of home architecture, was considered of utmost importance at this point in the development of Assisted Living as a building type, as opposed to simply providing direct illustrations of the considerations in place at an existing assisted living environment.

Concept of Home: Self-Projection/Self-Symbol

Identification

A place expressive of the identity of the unique individual and the status of the individual in the community.

Supportive Architectural Characteristics of Home

a) The home as a whole presents a unique and identifiable image. It supports the need to identify a specific place, space, and image as "yours" and "of you." (See Figures 4.1, 4.2.)

b) Home provides special places inside for which to display objects, and is made, in part, of special pieces that are meaningful themselves. (See Figure 4.3.)

Discussion

Clare Cooper-Marcus (1974) discusses the aspect of home as a symbol of self. The exterior facade reflects the identity one wants to express to the community—the status and image for others to identify you. The interior reflects the inner self—the image one wants to reflect or inspire to one's self. Together, these aspects reflect a public self and a personal self. Home enables us to project these images onto and into a concrete, tangible object.

Figure 4.1 *(Left) This coastal house presents a powerful and memorable image at its gable facade. (Reproduced with permission from Venturi, Rauch Scott-Brown, and Associates.)*

Figure 4.2 *(Below) This design involves a building where each grouping of spaces is enclosed in its own unique volume, as described in this elevation and section, creating identifiable spaces within a whole composition. (Reproduced with permission of Robert A.M. Stearn, Architects.)*

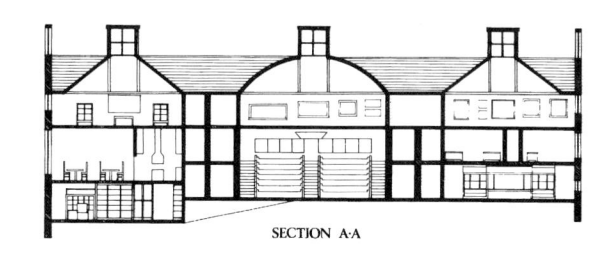

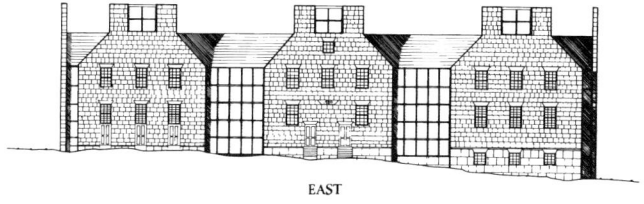

ARCHITECTURAL DESIGN CONSIDERATIONS

Figure 4.3 *This beautifully designed window seat is a special element at the window edge for storing and displaying items, as well as sitting.*

Architectural Implications

Accommodating these important notions of "home" implies creating a distinguishable whole, either standing alone or of distinct units within a larger collection of units. At a large scale this may be interpreted as interior or exterior window patterns or formal and figural facade treatments that suggest individual units. At a smaller scale, this may be a matter of considering and affording special places within to place and display important objects and artifacts (see also "Center/Origin").

1) Personalizable Entry

Definition

A personalizable entry has the potential for placement of personal items (e.g., photos, flowers and plants, wall hanging, knickknacks, etc), at the transition space between the more-public shared and circulation spaces and the more-private and personal residents' apartments. This also speaks of the clear demarcation of individual units within a whole complex.

Problem Statement

Repeated apartments along a corridor may become monotonous or confusing if they are undifferentiated from one another.

Thresholds between public and private space may not be clearly understood as such if there are no environmental cues that connect a particular individual with the private space beyond.

Discussion

Visitors may find it difficult to locate their friend's apartment, and residents with cognitive impairments may find it difficult to identify their own apartment from others' if apartments are undifferentiated and not clearly identified with a particular person. The use of nameplates attempts to accomplish this, but fails when the nameplates themselves are identical, lacking personality, and stirring institutional connotations of uniformity.

Circulation and apartment connections that do not offer some sort of alcove or layer space between them not only ignore the important transition between the two spaces, but do not afford residents any space to personalize and possess the entry as *their* entry.

Design Consideration

Consider layering the apartment entry off of the circulation system in a strong yet open manner that affords opportunities for personalization and speaks of the transition from shared space to private space. This could include an entry alcove that acts as an informal front porch to the circulation route, with views and connection to a courtyard or shared space (see Figure 4.4), an interior window between corridor and apartment with a sill for displaying items (see Figure 4.5), a personal display case on the corridor edge (see Figure 4.6), a shelf that accommodates plants, memorabilia, or a personal photo or image that carries meaning and identity to the resident.

Rationale

Opportunities for personalization can give each apartment "face" a unique identity as belonging to one particular resident with his/her

Figure 4.4 *(Below, left) This design for a housing complex includes a porch layer on the street, where chairs, plants, etc. could be placed, enabling personalization near unit entries. (Reproduced with permission of Machado Silvetti and Assoc.)*

Figure 4.5 *(Below, right) This built-in display piece at the entry into a resident's apartment provides a prominent place for residents to personalize their home.*

Figure 4.6 This design for an elderly cooperative includes a glass display box for resident use along the corridor edge. (From Elderly Housing Cooperative, William Brummett, Architect.)

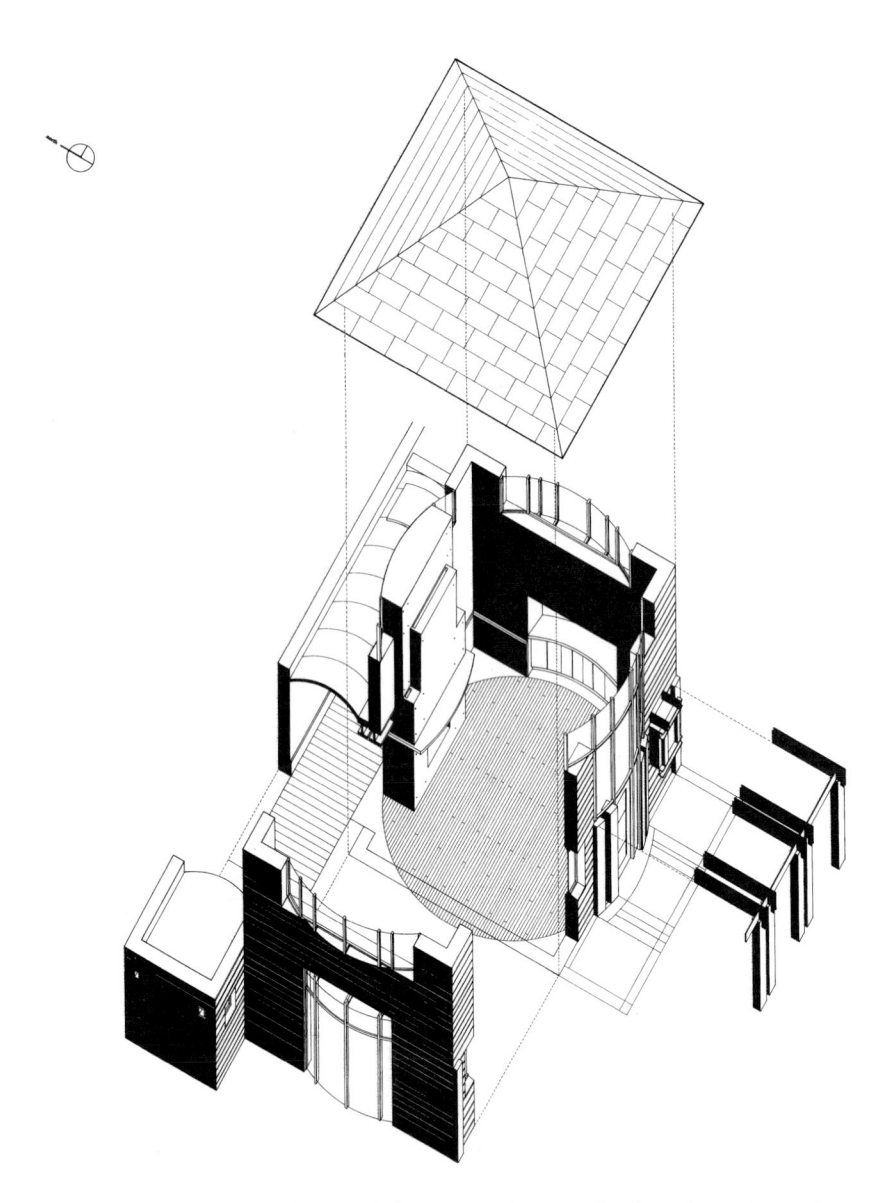

own, unique personality and history. The wayfinding benefits of unit entries with unique, personal character, orienting confused or cognitively impaired residents with meaningful cues describing apartment ownership and occupancy, are substantiated throughout current literature (Cohen and Weisman, 1991; Calkins, 1988; Regnier, 1991).

2) Deconstructed Corridors

Definition

Deconstructed corridors are circulation routes that are clear, yet potentially have a double identity and use by acting as spaces or edges for activity.

Problems Statement

The spatial quality of a corridor is loaded with institutional connotations, disorienting absence of differentiation and articulation, and lack of identity.

Discussion

Typical corridors that are double-loaded (i.e., rooms off of both sides of the corridor) provide little meaningful connection to the outdoors—a factor which has a great impact on orientation within a space. Similarly, long, repetitive, and unarticulated corridors may be confusing, as they provide no landmarks within which to orient oneself. Such corridors also speak of sameness with regard to apartments and residents, as opposed to uniqueness and individuality.

Particularly in double-loaded systems, the corridor is understood as a space in-between—a relative no-man's land that is not claimed, possessed, personalized, nor activated.

Design Consideration

This issue suggests two approaches to mitigating the negative image and behavioral effects of traditional long, double-loaded corridor systems.

The first approach is to consider the corridor a single-loaded edge between apartments and shared space, either exterior or interior. The corridor then becomes a place to develop porchlike conditions along the side of the corridor adjoining apartments. (See Figure 4.7.)

By looping around a central shared space or courtyard, the corridor also becomes a turning path with shorter continuous horizontal stretches.

A second approach, where it is necessary to have double-loaded corridor systems, is to curve or jog the corridor's path and interrupt the linearity of it with a variety of active and passive spaces. (See Figure 4.8.) Turns in the path need to be carefully weighed against path clarity to ensure clear and easy wayfinding.

Rationale

Corridor systems such as these can translate a long, undifferentiated and monotonous path into one with opportunities for interior views; passive and active engagement; renewed orientation to place, time of day, and year; and happenings within the facility (Regnier, 1992). Clarity in wayfinding can be enhanced also, as the path now

Figure 4.7 *(Below, left) Annie Maxim House is organized about a single-loaded corridor which curves to form a courtyard. (Barry Korobkin, Architect.)*

Figure 4.8 *(Below, right) This sitting space, created where two corridors meet, adds spatial variety and introduces an activity alcove along the corridor. (Rackleff House, Canby, Oregon. Chilles-Nielsen Architects.)*

has places, events, and landmarks along it that mark and pace the path. Finally, in single-loaded systems, the edge of the corridor nearest apartments can become part of the residents' territory off of their entry, encouraging passive use and personalization.

Concept of Home: Vessel of Memory/Vessel of Soul

A place where one finds the important and meaningful things one covets. It is a place of continuity, a place that holds memories.

Supportive Architectural Characteristics of Home

a) Home is embedded with a variety of levels of scale and detail, presenting a rich bouquet of interest and stimulation. A fine texture and scale of detail is developed that holds beauty and interest, and speaks of the materials and construction, and the fact that human hands shaped it. (See Figures 4.9, 4.10.)

b) Home provides special opportunities, elements, and places that allow the owner to place meaningful items for display and enrichment.

Figure 4.9 (Below, left) The level of detail and articulation in this house speaks of care and intimacy with the environment of home. (Reproduced with permission of Bethany Christenson-Puopolo, Architect.)

Figure 4.10 (Below, right) This finely detailed corner reflects the care and attention expected in the design of one's home. (Rosewood Estates, Roseville, Minn. BRW Elness Architects.)

Discussion

The sterility of institutional environs is due in part to an overwhelming uniformity and lack of detail. These characteristics address the value of variety, scale, and detail. Home is an environment with which the inhabitants become intimate. Such refinement ensures that even over time and with familiarity, home remains a place of beauty and interest, complete, whole, finished, evocative, and inspiring.

Architectural Implications

The naturally occurring joints, transitions, and trims of a building, such as openings in walls, and corners and edges, can become opportunities for special treatments and refinements.

Definition

Material quality and spatial character speaks to the visual, referential, volumetric, and tactile characteristics of the spaces and finish materials. These often are the elements that residents come in close contact with or view up close.

Problem Statement

Typical institutional materials, finishes, and details (such as undifferentiated, continuous, shiny beige composition floor tile) convey a powerful message of lack of care, illness, and discomfort (Lindsay, 1991).

Discussion

Particularly for residents with limited sensory or cognitive abilities, the things close at hand can speak the loudest about the character of the environment. If the overriding concerns are that these materials and details speak only of durability, low cost and low maintenance, then they will likely speak of institution, where such issues are typically paramount.

Design Consideration

Consider the exterior materials and detailing to reflect the qualities of homes in the context that speak of the place as a residence, within a specific context with unique resources, mannerisms, and traditions. (See Figure 4.11.)

Built-in furnishings or special elements, such as bookshelves in a library, living room, den, or resident apartment; a china cabinet in a dining room; cabinetry in a kitchen; or a fireplace in the main space or dining room, should all be of a fine level of detail. (See Figure 4.12.)

Lighting should be incandescent to emit a warm-light quality, and indirect or shaded to prevent glare, as many residents may be particularly sensitive to glare or be overstimulated by harsh light. Wall-mounted, ceiling-hung, valance, or table top lamp fixtures in general should be considered in lieu of fluorescent fixtures.

Domestic plumbing fixtures of high durability, such as sinks, toilets, bathroom mirrors, and showers, should be used in place of institutional fixtures whenever possible. Attention must be paid to specifying domestic fixtures that are accessible.

3) Refined Material Quality and Spatial Character

Rationale

The intention here is not to imply that a building should mimic an older house or house type. Rather, the qualities of the details and materials of such should be understood as design impetus from which to arrive at solutions unique to the conditions of the project.

If a place is to be understood and accepted by residents as home, at a daily and intimate level, it must carry the warm, engaging, comfortable, and beautiful qualities of it.

In some instances, the benefit of durability may have to be weighed against the value of an element's contribution to a homelike environment. Recent developments in material durabilities and extended material palettes offer new potential for meeting the long-term cost and maintenance demands while maintaining homelike ambiance.

4) Refined Scale

Definition

Scale is a product of articulation, not size. The refinement of such refers to a high level of layered or embedded architectural relationships between the whole and its parts.

Problem Statement

Large-scaled or singularly scaled buildings (ones with only one level of articulation—the building as a whole) do not reflect the intimate relationship people have with their home.

Discussion

A building as such ignores the realization that home is engaged at many levels and distances (most of which are very close), and for very long periods of time. A building with little or no scale is more difficult to understand and orient within and about, and is of little interest or enriching potential (Norburg-Schulz, 1985).

Figure 4.11 *(Below, left) The formality of the composition of this turn-of-the-century Chicago house suggests its urbane and sophisticated context. A finely detailed stone facade speaks of the natural resource—limestone—once available in the area.*

Figure 4.12 *(Below, right) The fireplace at Annie Maxim House.*

Design Consideration

Consider the elements of the building as working together to translate the overall composition of the building into human-related pieces and features. Building pieces, layers, window openings and panes, door openings, finish materials, and details, should be of increasingly more human-related size and refinement. Particular attention should be concentrated at points of resident contact with the building and frequent use, such as entries, porches, transition spaces, places of rest, and resident rooms. (See Figures 4.13, 4.14.)

Rationale

By reducing the scale, the abstraction of the entire building is powerfully transformed into a place of human interaction and occupation. The size of things is then understood in terms of relationships of smaller, understandable elements (moldings, casings, doors, windows, etc.) to larger ones (room volumes, facade pieces, etc.) and to one's self.

Concept of Home: Connectedness/Belonging

A place offering meaningful connections with family and community, where one is a valuable contributor to a greater whole.

Supportive Architectural Characteristics of Home

a) Home is sighted within a relative and known relationship and proximity to peers (Rowe, 1991). In an urban context, this distance may be a few feet. (See Figure 4.15.) In a rural context, this distance may be many miles. However, there is a known, expected, and logical system. (See Figure 4.16.)

Figure 4.13 *(Below, left) The pergola at the Graves Residence brings an intimate and delicate scale to its garden facade. (Reproduced with permission of Michael Graves, Architects.)*

Figure 4.14 *(Below, right) A high level of refinement along a sitting edge at the entry stairs to Rob Krier's Seaside house.*

b) Home generally conforms to the accepted design pattern of the context, yet with variations, adaptations, and modifications. These modifications respond to needs or specific circumstance. (See Figure 4.17.) This allows home to be both part of the pattern and specific to owner (Jackson, 1985).

c) Community-engaging semitransparent spaces are formed along the most public realm of home allowing the double reading of one's own space and communal space. (See Figure 4.18.)

Discussion

The ability of a home (and the person within it) to be recognized and identified as part of an important community, one with established patterns and processes, is an important intention. The home can be considered a physical manifestation of the dual nature of living in the community, both as an individual and a member of an important group.

Architectural Implications

By no means does this imply a simple or literal mimicking of homes in the context. Rather, this underscores the importance of studying and understanding the overall planning, siting, and formal, figural, and material qualities and opportunities of a given site. A context's residential fabric, general proportioning systems, siting patterns, ordering and circulating systems, levels of transparency to the street, and sequences from the street to the interior may suggest directions for design.

Figure 4.15 *(Below, left) This aerial rendering of a housing complex shows a clear ordering of houses about streets and circles. (Reproduced with permission of Robert A.M. Stearn, Architects.)*

Figure 4.16 *(Below, right) A typical farmhouse pattern of open yard to the south, house gable facing the street, and barn or workhouse between work yard and fields is an accepted pattern known to work successfully.*

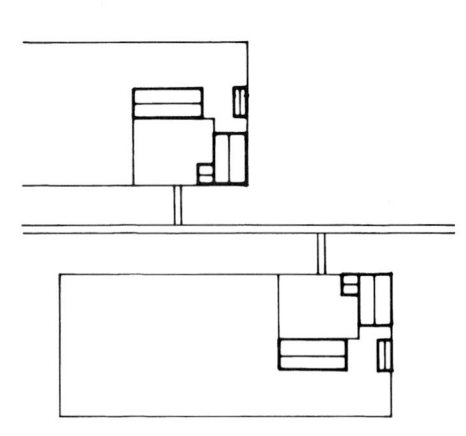

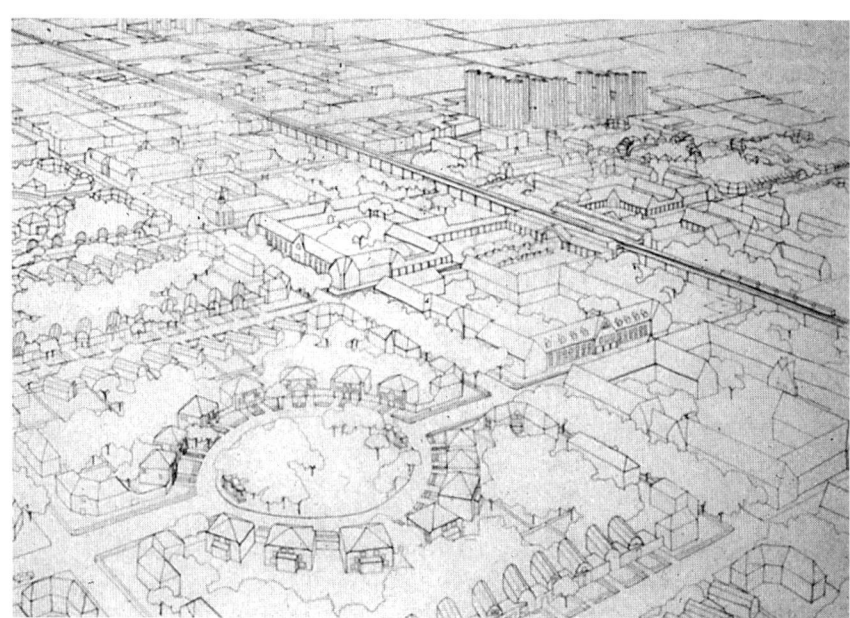

5) Community-Integrated Sites

Definition

Community-integrated sites are connected by location, operation, and supporting architecture to the social and commercial workings of a community.

Problem Statement

Relocation of a resident from his or her long-time independent home can represent a tremendous loss of belonging to a community, and the ability to partake in activities that reinforce this belonging. Facilities that do not physically or operationally attempt to foster such belonging may tend to isolate residents from a meaningful and enjoyable peer group, and valuable community activity and resources.

Discussion

Site selection is often a given by the time architects are first commissioned for projects. Sophisticated developers, however, aware of the complex and competitive Assisted Living marketplace, frequently engage the services of architects as special consultants during initial feasibility and planning studies.

Isolated and segregated sites offer little in terms of community engagement, even with occasional planned and chauffeured excursions. Under such situations, important connections to, and identification with, a community may be lost. The important variety of levels of experience from home to community may be greatly reduced by a very limited accessible domain.

Design Consideration

Consider sites located within a short (and safe) walking distance to commercial and social places such as restaurants, markets, churches, retail shops, parks, and other community facilities. (See Figure 4.19.)

Figure 4.17 *(Below, left) Houses fronting a pedestrian walkway, with some variety in setback and approach, Seaside, Florida.*

Figure 4.18 *(Below, right) A semi-transparent porch layer along a street edge. (Reproduced with permission of Scott Merrill, Architect.)*

6) Stages for Community Interaction

Rationale

Assisted living facilities that are sited within a working community system can provide opportunities for connections that extend far beyond the facility itself (Hoglund, 1985). Such opportunities also foster resident independence, potentially freeing the more physically capable residents from having to rely on others to deliver needed goods or shuttle them about from the facility to distant destinations.

Definition

Stages for community interaction refers to physical and operational settings within the facility, accessible to all, which act as common ground for residents, visitors, and other members of the community.

Problem Statement

Many assisted living residents may have mobility, cognitive, or other frailties or impairments that make it difficult for them to travel outside of the facility. Yet the need to connect with and engage others outside of their home does not diminish with decreasing abilities.

Discussion

Those with mobility-limiting impairments often become relatively isolated from their greater community because of this inability to access it. Conversely, the community also becomes isolated from many of its elders through a lack of common ground. The enrichment potentials for both groups in terms of social, educational, and cultural exchanges are lessened by such lack of setting in which to engage.

Design Consideration

Include in the programming and design of assisted living facilities a commercial, retail, service entity, or other small-scaled public place for stimulating resident-community interaction. The definition of the public place depends largely on the scale and scope of the particular facility and appropriate response to the context.

Smaller (20–60 units) or stand-alone facilities could offer places, such as a cafe, bakery, bookstore, coffee house, or general store, which work as inviting, meaningful, and active additions to the community fabric. (See Figure 4.20.)

Larger facilities, buildings in isolated contexts, dense urban facilities, or those part of a larger CCRC campus could include a meeting hall or larger group activity space that could serve community groups.

This public accommodation should be located at the most-public edge or portion of the site, and developed to invite those who do not reside in the facility. Entry to this public space should be clearly separate and distinct from entry to the facility itself.

A careful layering system should be considered at the threshold

Figure 4.19 *A public cafe adjacent to a European assisted living facility.*

Figure 4.20 *This assisted living facility includes an ice cream parlor within the facility, as a normalized and engaging social setting.*

between the commercial space and the rest of the facility, with the intent of providing easy and clear resident access, yet cueing appropriate public/private approaches and behaviors.

The character of the space should be understood as a special commercial space within a residence.

Rationale

Providing such settings establishes the facility as a productive, active, and engaging member of the community, and enhances residents' opportunities to be meaningful contributors to the community family of which they are a part.

The establishment of a working component within the facility provides residents with new access to meaningful occupational therapy. It may be possible for some of the residents to assist in the operation of the public component, fostering a sense of connection, purpose, value, and self-worth. Regnier (1992) discusses European Assisted Living prototypes where such components occur and are successful.

Even at a modest scale, a place within the facility that has the identity as both part of the facility and part of the community provides a more public (yet casual) setting, for social interaction with other residents, visitors, and patrons, and accommodates interesting people-watching activity. For residents who have more debilitating mobility or cognitive impairments, such a place can present an enjoyable change of pace and environment, without necessitating extensive assistance in accessing it.

Definition

An area where residents' mailboxes are grouped, which affords comfortable and casual socialization and access at any time, initiates a mailbox event.

7) MAILBOX EVENT

ARCHITECTURAL DESIGN CONSIDERATIONS   53

Problem Statement

In many institutional settings, resident mail is delivered to a caregiver, and then distributed to residents at the discretion and convenience of the caregiver, or according to a preset mail-pickup time. Such procedures, and the architecture that accommodates them, denies residents of their rights of accessibility, individuality in routine, and privacy concerning their correspondence.

Discussion

Handling mail in this manner converts the normal event of receiving daily correspondence into another element of staff control and potentially demeaning and arbitrary routine.

In a small yet meaningful way, residents' free and independent access to their own mail supports many of the definitive philosophies of Assisted Living, such as resident control, dignity, privacy, and independence, and respects residents as whole and capable individuals with inalienable rights and responsibilities.

Design Consideration

Locate mailboxes in a space adjacent to the main gathering space, in a manner that affords and encourages casual socialization around the

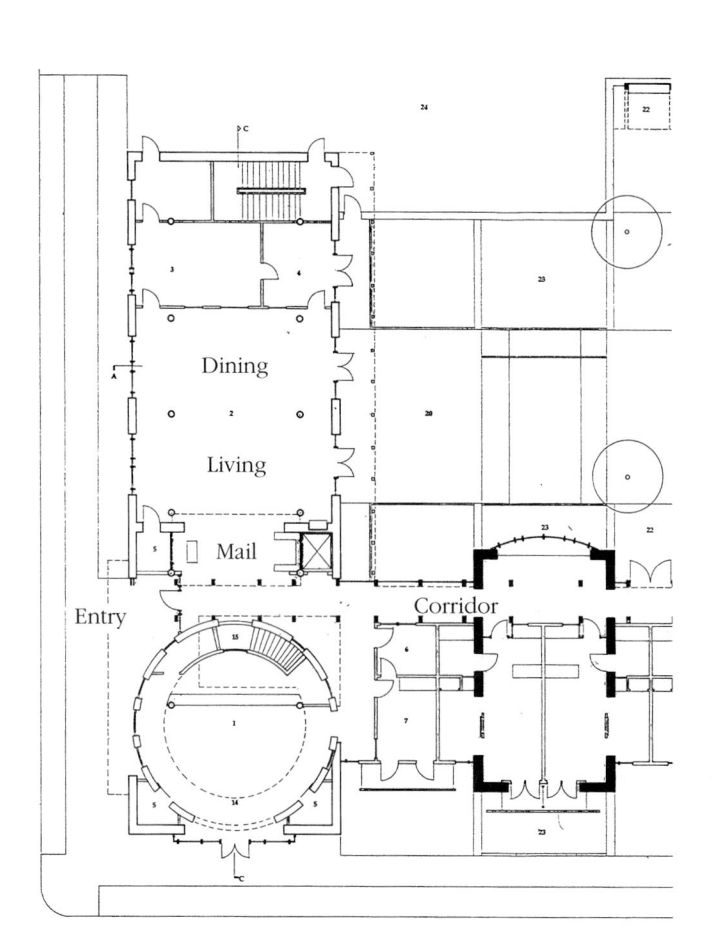

Figure 4.21 *Mailboxes are located at the area of highest circulation and adjacent to, and in view of, a number of active areas, in this assisted living design. (From Corvallis Assisted Living, William Brummett, Architect.)*

event of receiving mail. (See Figure 4.21.) Residents should have personal keys to their boxes, and be afforded unlimited access to them.

Rationale

For some residents, particularly those who have more severe physical or cognitive limitations, mail may be one of the few connections to the world beyond the facility, and perhaps also to family and friends living in distant locations. The affordance and encouragement of the anticipation and event surrounding mail delivery could provide them with opportunities for meaningful activity and socialization, as well as providing a routine-orienting event that marks the time of day and year. Personal locks and unlimited access fosters residents' sense of control, autonomy, and independence, and reinforces the understanding of the place as *their* home.

8) Disguised, Minimized, and Decentralized Parking

Definition

Disguised, minimized, and decentralized parking refers to parking lots that are visually obscured and divided into smaller groupings of parking spaces.

Problem Statement

Most assisted living facilities must provide some on-site parking for staff and visitors. Unfortunately, the appearance of a parking lot full of cars is generally inconsistent with the typical approach, density, and pattern of parking cars within a residential neighborhood.

Discussion

In some dense urban settings, a parking lot may be part of the normal pattern among apartment towers. In most assisted living settings, however, the appearance of a large, dense parking lot fronting a building that is supposed to be residential represents a foreign intrusion in the context, and could present an undesirable public or institutional character.

Design Consideration

Design small parking lots or divide the necessary area into a number of smaller lots, which are located to the side or toward the rear of the site, to minimize the impact of a lot from the street front and building approach. (See Figure 4.22.) Landscape design measures, to disguise parking lots and automobiles, such as screening with plantings, berms, portions of the building, and natural contours of the site, should be employed. Since few assisted living residents drive, a minimum number of parking spaces for staff and visitors should be considered and advocated to the local building official.

Figure 4.22 *Parking divided into a number of smaller lots and pushed to the rear of the site at Rosewood Estates. (Reproduced with permission of BRW Elness, Assoc.)*

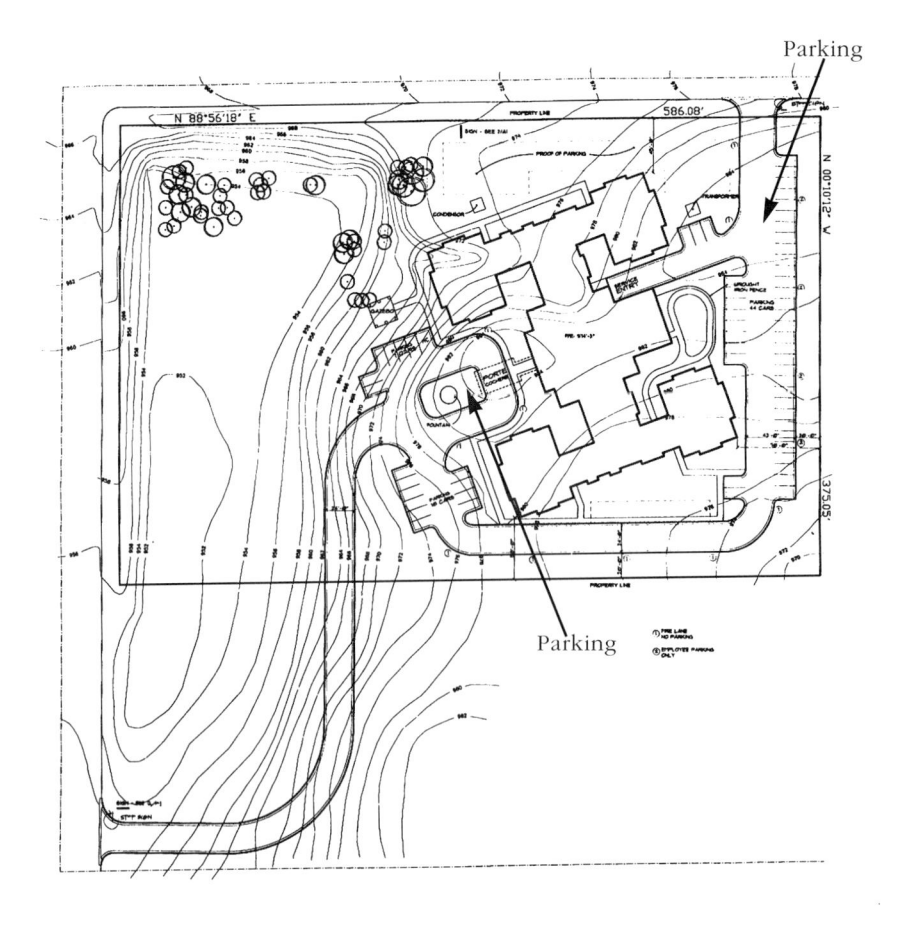

Rationale

An approach to parking design that considers smaller groupings of a few cars and veiling the lot itself with landscaping can minimize the impact of a larger building in a residential neighborhood, and represents one of the elements of presenting a whole character of residentiality (Lui, 1992).

ORIENTATION

CONCEPT OF HOME: CENTER/ORIGIN

A fixed center from which to embark and to which to return.

Supportive Architectural Characteristics of Home

The composition of home forms a complete and identifiable figure, marking a solid, stable, identifiable, and human-scaled landmark. (See Figure 4.23.)

Discussion

The home is the center of the physical world (Cooper-Marcus, 1974). Each person lives a life "radiating from home." Without a clear, identifiable, fixed center, our primary orientation to the world is absent. We are lost, both physically and psychologically.

Figure 4.23 *This log cabin by architect Ron Mason reads as a "lantern" standing in the dense and dark Colorado woods.*

Architectural Implications

This principle underscores the importance of the home as a personal landmark, or icon, recognizable as one's own spatial touchstone. This implies an architectural description, development, and accommodation that allows each home to "read" relatively distinct and complete. Also, this concept further suggests the importance of affording the resident places and elements for personalizing his or her home.

9) Articulated Mass and Form

Definition

Articulated mass and form involves a literal (real) or phenomenal (perceived) break in plane, material, finish, and/or detail in order to delineate pieces, as well as the whole, as complete objects.

Problem Statement

Unarticulated residential buildings the size of assisted living facilities are usually understood as something other than a residence, since no piece/articulation of the building relates to a realm reasonably and comfortably occupied and understood by, or unique and related to, an individual.

ARCHITECTURAL DESIGN CONSIDERATIONS   57

Figure 4.24 *This large apartment complex in Amsterdam is beautifully articulated by modules of back-to-back apartments.*

Discussion

An assisted living facility with articulated mass and form is one in which the architectural composition speaks of the nature of the building—a grouping of shared spaces and apartments of unique individuals, as opposed to a uniform and undifferentiated institution.

A lack of articulation can also make orientation for residents and visitors more difficult, as there are fewer spatial cues and landmarks.

Design Consideration

Consider the overall form as groupings of smaller pieces that relate to individual apartments, apartment groupings or clusters, and special rooms within, as an approach that could support the identity and image of the facility as a residence. This can also provide smaller, identifiable, and manageable clusters of spaces from within. (See Figure 4.24.) This articulation could take place as either substantial dimensional changes in plan or phenomenal layering of the wall plane.

It is often important for this articulation to occur both in the wall plane (through such elements as clustering of units, creating bays, layering edges, or creating a base), and in the roof form (by employing changes in eave, parapet and ridge lines, succinct roof pieces over clusters or groupings, or a breaking of the roof with such elements as dormers).

In smaller facilities in small community, suburban, or rural settings, cues can be taken from homes in the context that suggest appropriate proportional, dimensional, and figural qualities of the interrelation of the features.

In more dense, urban settings with high-rise apartments, articulation of bays, balconies, and special window features can provide means to such differentiation.

Rationale

The issues here are ones of figural identity and scale. By articulating the mass, it is possible for even a larger building to convey an image and character that is homelike. On the other hand, a building of unusual size or mass, uniform and undifferentiated in a meaningful manner, could create an image irreconcilable with home.

CONCEPT OF HOME: PRIVACY/TERRITORIALITY

A place of rest, intimacy, and solitude: a place that is yours with clear boundaries.

Supportive Architectural Characteristics of Home

a) Clear realms of semipublic to private space are delineated within the home with layers, or a contrast between open and closed rooms (Norberg-Schultz, 1985) (See Figure 4.25.)

b) Home marks its territory at the site edge. This usually occurs with landscape elements, fences, steps, or simply a pristine lawn (Metre, 1983) (See Figures 4.26, 4.27.)

Discussion

The control of the interface between the inner private realm of the home and the outer public realm enables home to be owned in a literal and conceptual sense. The clarity of the transition which happens at this interface physically describes the public and private domains, and cues the appropriate behaviors about them.

Figure 4.25 *This view of a design for elderly housing shows a transparent (glass) porch and window seats, contrasted by smaller and deeper openings in a thick masonry wall which conceal more private spaces beyond. (From Elderly Housing Cooperative, William Brummett, Architect.)*

Figure 4.26 (Above, left) *A lamppost and manicured lawn mark the edge of this site.*

Figure 4.27 (Above, right) *This house employs a classic picket fence to clearly mark a shallow front yard.*

Architectural Implications

The consideration of appropriate (and locally known and accepted) architectural demarcations and transitions from one space with one kind of character and activity, to another space with another kind of ambiance, begins to address this issue (Scott-Brown, 1977). This may often imply a series of transitions that carefully unfold and accept. This also suggests an overall clarity in planning which describes what realms are private, shared, and public.

10) Private Apartments

Definition

Private apartments are single-occupancy apartments with private living, sleeping, bathing, and meal preparation areas.

Problem Statement

Shared apartments significantly compromise a resident's ability to experience private and intimate activity, and personalize and possess his/her home.

Discussion

Sharing one's own private space with another (except by choice, as in the case of a couple) limits the activity one can undertake. Quiet or intimate activity may be impossible with another person in the room, or knowledge that a roommate may soon interrupt.

Furthermore, significant differences in sleeping, eating, grooming, housekeeping, or social activity may also compromise one's sense of control, stability, and autonomy with regard to lifestyle and daily routine.

Design Consideration

Design apartments as single occupancy. A small proportion of two-bedroom/two-occupant apartments may be considered in the overall design for the few residents who may wish to live with a spouse, relative, or companion. However, all residents, regardless of financial resources, must have the right and ability to live in a single-occupancy apartment.

Rationale

The only reasonable space for truly private or intimate activity is one's own private apartment.

Many contemporary assisted living facilities offer a small number of "private lounges" with the intent of being used privately by any resident as desired. Unfortunately, these rooms belong to no one *and* anyone, negating any feeling of connectedness or security that is important for meaningful intimate or contemplative activity.

Sharing one's private space with another (by default, not by choice) thoroughly undermines many of the conceptual notions of home, is in complete opposition to many of the therapeutic goals of Assisted Living, and is therefore absolutely unacceptable.

11) Clear Thresholds

Definition

Thresholds are the "lines" or "realms" that distinguish one space and way of being/acting/behaving from another.

Problem Statement

Unclear transitions between one place or activity and another results in an ambiguous distinction between the two, with equally ambiguous understandings of appropriate behavior.

Discussion

Many assisted living residents have impairments causing a reduced ability to clearly comprehend their environment. An unclear physical environment can compound this misunderstanding, potentially increasing confusion, anxiety, inappropriate behavior, and dependency on caregiving staff (Brawley, 1992).

Design Consideration

Consider clear and significant architectural changes to clearly mark transitions from one realm to another. These may include differences in detail, material, scale, volume, light, texture, rhythm, or opacity. (See Figure 4.28.)

Rationale

Of all behavioral and environmental cues offered through architecture, the threshold from one realm to another is among the most important and powerful. It cues a real and perceived change not only

Figure 4.28 *A powerful change in scale and character in this Frank Israel house addition creates a dramatic threshold at the entrance from one realm of the house to another.*

in space, but also expectations and norms regarding behavior and activity (Thiis-Evensen, 1989).

Clear thresholds mark this transition as the important place where such a transformation in ambiance and attitude takes place.

12) Separate Living and Sleeping Areas

Definition

This consideration refers to a clear division between a sleeping area and living area within each resident apartment.

Problem Statement

Social space and bedroom space are usually culturally incompatible. Without separate living and sleeping areas, the important distinction between these two disparate functions becomes ambiguous. In most cases where such a division is not made, either the resident's bedroom becomes a semipublic social space and the resident has no private space, or the living room becomes the bedroom, and the resident must leave the apartment to socialize in comfort.

Discussion

Privacy, choice, dignity, and control are central issues here that are supported by affording residents the opportunity to veil their most private area when others are visiting in the apartment.

Visitors may be discouraged from meeting residents in their apartments by awkward feelings of invading the resident's own private bedroom.

62   THE ESSENCE OF HOME

Design Consideration

Provide a means of separating the sleeping area from the living area within apartments. This separation should be flexible and adaptable to allow a resident to easily separate or connect the two areas visually.

In larger apartments, this may involve a separate bedroom with a wide opening between the two rooms that could be closed by a system of French, pocket, or windowed doors. (See Figure 4.29.)

In smaller apartments, this may take the form of an ample alcove separated from the living area by a similar system of French doors, lightweight shutters, semitransparent screens, or a beautiful and tactile curtain or tapestry. (See Figure 4.30.)

Rationale

In addition to issues of privacy, control, and dignity, the ability to separate the two areas also provides residents with options regarding which people see their sleeping areas. The ability to easily manipulate the level of separation and visual access takes into account issues of preview and control to and from the sleeping area. This also affords confused or cognitively-impaired residents the ability to open up divisions and connect the two areas for clarity and orientation.

Figure 4.29 *(Left) Large pocket doors afford variable levels of connection between these two rooms at Richardson's Glessner House.*

Figure 4.30 *(Below) French doors dividing two living spaces from one another.*

13) Backyard Realm

Definition

Backyard realm refers to the defined exterior room or rooms that are relatively private to the facility, are shared by the residents, and serve as a setting for informal outdoor gatherings.

Problem Statement

Because of physical, psychological, and cognitive frailties, many residents in assisted living facilities may not be able to enjoy the outdoors in an open or unprotected space.

Discussion

Those with physical frailties may be very fearful that a fall or accident outdoors or far beyond the facility will not be seen and tended to promptly, and are often concerned that their infirmities will target them as easy prey for those with devious intentions, aware of the residents' vulnerabilities.

Those with cognitive impairments may wander or become confused or disoriented in an open and undefined outdoor space (Calkins, 1988).

The experience of shared outdoor activity can provide meaningful connections to home and home activity, and provide an orientation to the time of day and year.

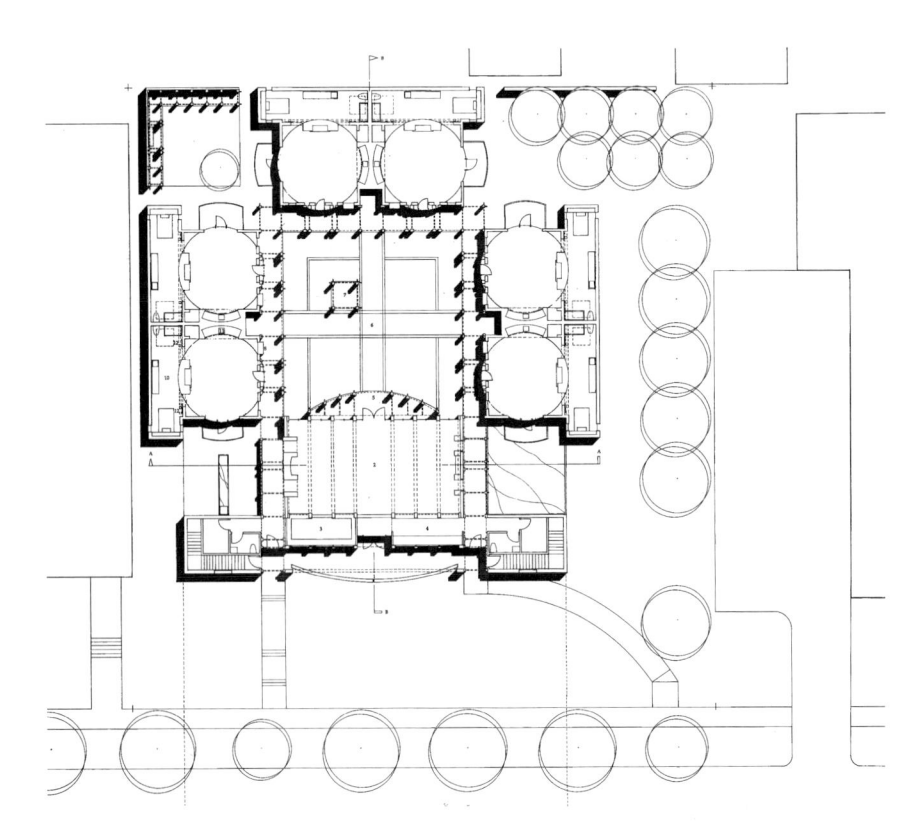

Figure 4.31 *Individual units face a courtyard protected from the busy street. (From Elderly Housing Cooperative, William Brummett, Architect.)*

Design Consideration

Through a combination of building and site design, form a defined, resident-shared outdoor space that is clearly a part of the residents' territory, and which is under resident control. The nature, scale, and character of this backyard may vary greatly according to the scale of the facility and the context of which it is a part. Possible manifestations include a courtyard (see Figure 4.31), a backyard partially or fully enclosed by landscaping and fencing (see Figure 4.32), developed space between buildings or wings of a building (see Figure 4.33), or a large deck. (See Figure 4.34.) The design of these spaces should be purposeful and eventful, and provide and suggest opportunities for active and passive social, occupational, and therapeutic activity.

Rationale

By establishing a backyard realm somewhat sheltered from the outer world, an outdoor place is created for residents that is consistent with the opportunities of activity afforded in a home and that supports relaxed and casual activity and socialization, such as sitting and talking in the shade, picnicking, barbecuing, or gardening.

Figure 4.32 *This south-facing courtyard is completed by a pergola and line of trees along its south side, creating a safe, semiprivate environment shielded from the alley beyond. (From Corvallis Assisted Living.)*

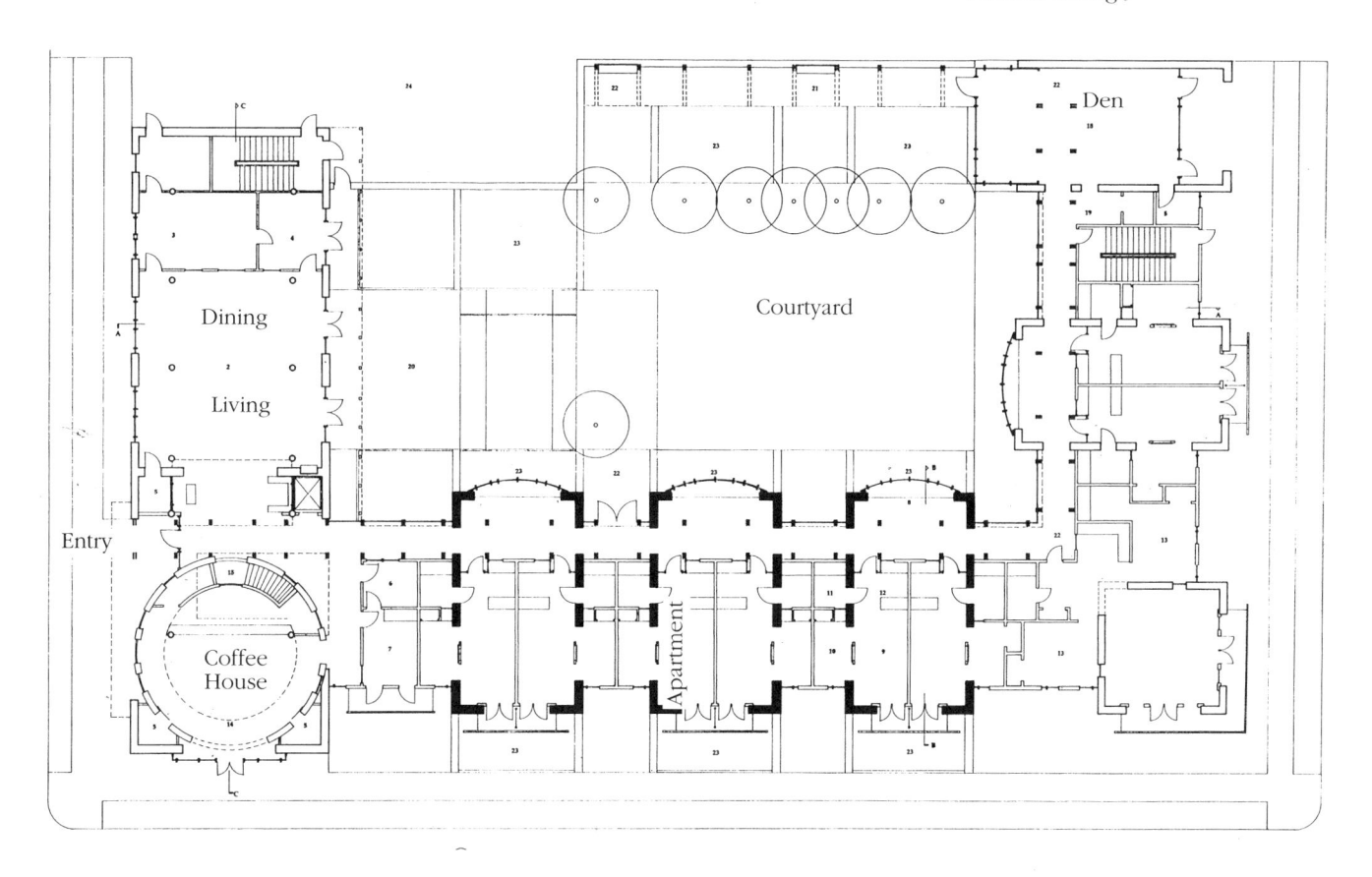

ARCHITECTURAL DESIGN CONSIDERATIONS

Figure 4.33 *(Right) As this Norwegian assisted living facility conforms to a difficult site, it forms a triangular atria within.*

Figure 4.34 *(Below, right) A deck overlooking the woods and distant lake at Sunrise Retirement Home of Mercer Island, Washington.*

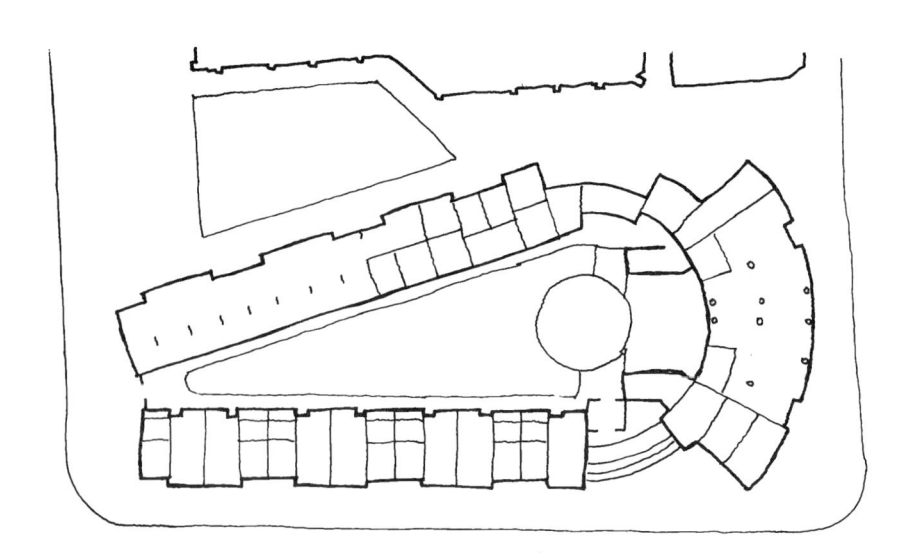

14) Modified Delivery Place and System

Definition

Modified delivery place and system refers to a noninstitutional and unobtrusive space and method of receiving goods and supplies.

Problem Statement

Although assisted living facilities do require some regular delivery of goods and supplies, the regular intrusion of delivery personnel may very well represent an infringement on personal territory and routine.

Discussion

An important notion to one's sense of territoriality is a sense of control over the admittance of visitors. Frequently occurring, unexpected deliveries could undermine this important sense. Deliveries of goods, particularly to larger facilities and components within a CCRC

66 THE ESSENCE OF HOME

campus, can potentially become large-scale institutional disturbances. Those with dementia may become disoriented by the quick comings and goings of the delivery personnel and the noises the delivery process creates. Also, their attention may be unwittingly drawn toward an exit.

Design Consideration

Two approaches, or combinations of the two, provide guidance for the design and location of the necessary delivery place in facilities of various scales and contexts.

For smaller facilities, or for facilities in small community or rural settings, a side or back tertiary entry system designed as a "mud room," adjacent to the staff kitchen and storage, can provide an appropriate place and character for the small-scale deliveries that typically take place. (See Figure 4.35.) A door buzzer connected to the kitchen and reception could notify staff of delivery arrivals.

In larger facilities, or in facilities in harsh climates, a residential-like garage component adjacent to the kitchen and storage could accept vans and similar light trucks in a protected, enclosed environment consistent with the image and character of "home." (See Figure 4.36.)

Rationale

The intent is to minimize the nature, scale, and building system that accommodates the image and event of deliveries, to the extent that they become slightly modified, casual, homelike occurrences.

Concept of Home: Familiarity/Order

A place that is known, expected, and stable.

Concept of Home: Stability/Predictability

A place of comfort and inhibition, where locations and relationships are known and expected.

Figure 4.35 *(Below, left) The service entry at Rosewood.*

Figure 4.36 *(Below, right) Elder Homestead uses a residential-like garage as its point of service entry. (Reproduced with permission of BRW Elness, Assoc.)*

Supportive Architectural Characteristics of Home

a) Home is ordered and structured (although informally so) in a manner that is understood (Tillich, 1933). Usual orders may include: division of public and private realms, centripetal or linear spatial arrangement, and division and expression of function. Arrangements, locations, sizes, and relationships of rooms and elements are determined according to a slowly evolving tradition and practice where the basic order is constant, and small changes are made according to specific circumstance and incremental evolution. (See Figure 4.37.)

b) The composition of home forms a complete and identifiable figure. Its place, arrangement, and image are whole and known (see Figure 4.38) (Norburg-Schulz, 1985).

Discussion

The home presents an image and architectural language of a stable and comprehensive place. It will stand and protect, and is a complete and known icon.

Architectural Implications

An important consideration here is the architectural description of "home" as a logical and complete structural, spatial, organizational, circulatory, and material system.

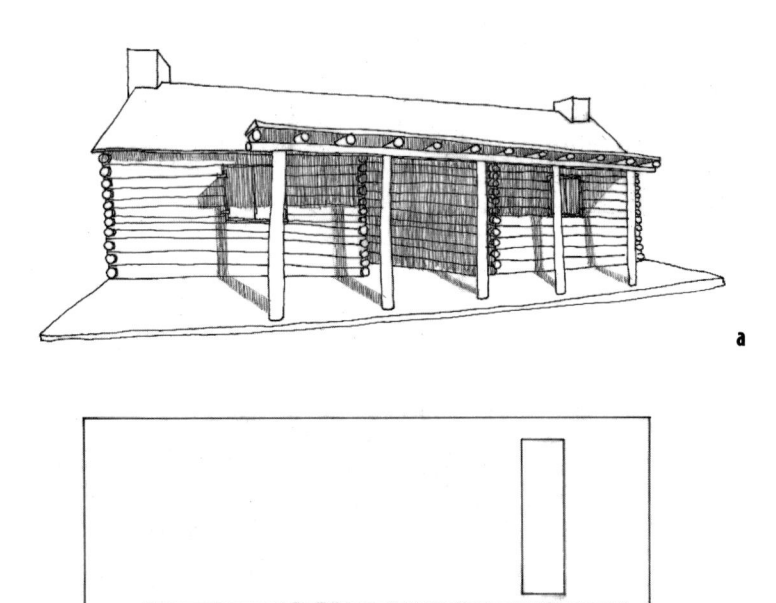

Figure 4.37 a & b *These images of a historic and contemporary house show a theme, the dogtrot house, proven to perform, which has evolved to its contemporary rendition. (Drawing: Nahum House, William Brummett, Architect.)*

68 THE ESSENCE OF HOME

15) Clear and Redundant Order

Definition

A building organization that is well defined, hierarchical, and reiterated through many different building elements is clear and appropriately redundant.

Problem Statement

Physical and cognitive impairments often diminish or limit a resident's ability to understand the organization of a built environment.

Discussion

Clarity in wayfinding is an important design consideration in Assisted Living, which is particularly salient when considering those with sensory or cognitive disabilities (Cohen and Weisman, 1991).

An unclear organization or building order may compound such problems, limiting a person's ability to independently navigate a facility and reach desired destinations and activities. The need to seek assistance in wayfinding could be detrimental to one's sense of dignity, control, and self-reliance.

In addition, an unclear order may necessitate visitors having to seek direction in order to find a friend's room or a desired shared space, thereby compromising the casual and familiar ambiance of the place.

Design Consideration

As a general concept, this consideration applies to the whole of the building organization.

Figure 4.38 *The Croffead House by Clark & Meneffee stands as an icon along the river which distinguishes its site.*

Consider making destinations, the nature of spaces, and routes and paths very clear and comprehensible. The articulation of the order should involve a range of architectural elements that work together to reinforce the understanding of the order of the building. (See Figure 4.39.)

Identifiable landmarks, clear thresholds, changes in ceiling height and light quality, changes in wall and floor finishes, and short, simple, and direct circulation routes with views to destination areas are among the strategies that could be employed.

Redundant cues with regard to orientation, order, and activity such as the aroma of baked goods and coffee prior to a breakfast, or music prior to an event can be expressed in ways involving all senses to compensate for those with sensory impairments. (See Figure 4.40.)

The creation of a central gathering space or main circulation crossing can provide an important and easily remembered center to a building. (See Figure 4.41.)

Rationale

The clear understanding of home promotes feelings of security, control, stability, autonomy, territoriality, permanence, and connectedness (Rapaport, 1967). Clarity and redundancy in design is a first step toward alleviating potential confusion and anxiety which may occur if an environment is difficult to comprehend.

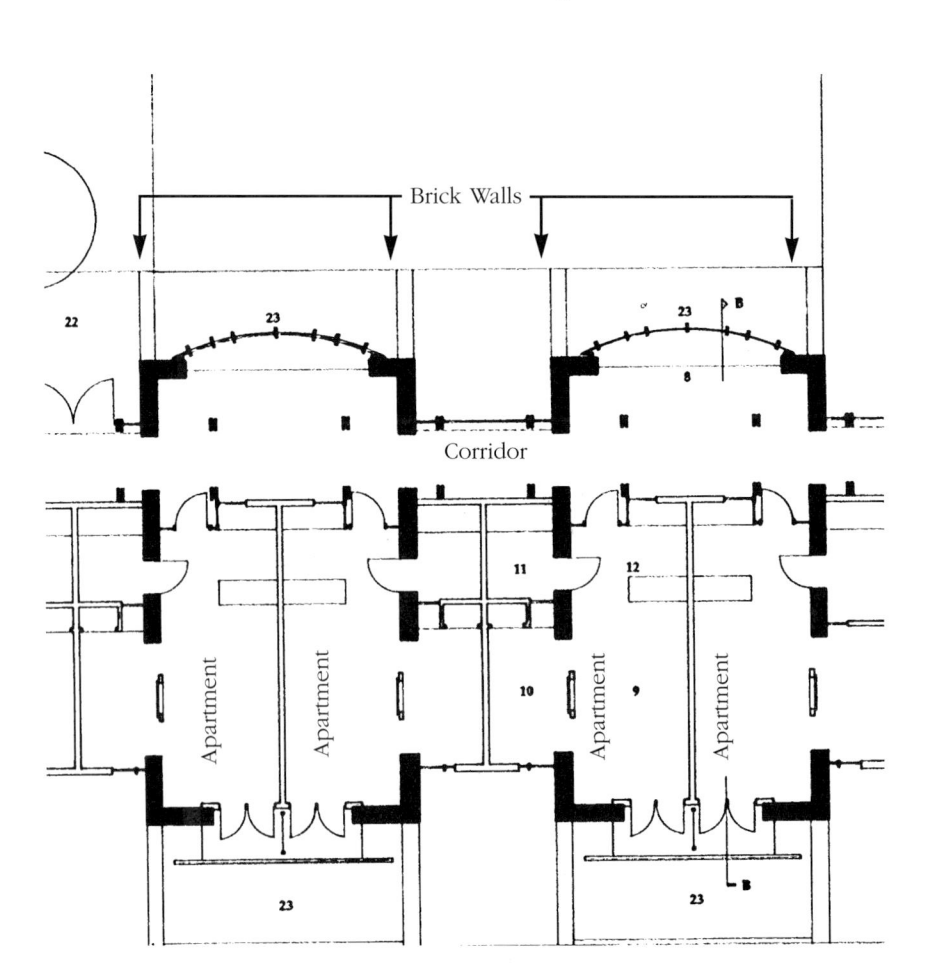

Figure 4.39 *Each bay of two apartments in this design for an assisted living facility is composed of thick brick walls which come into the corridor. The contrast between the corridor glass walls and the apartment brick walls provides an architectural cue that can orient residents as they walk along the corridor.*

70   THE ESSENCE OF HOME

Figure 4.40 *A piano is offered in the main living room at Annie Maxim House.*

Figure 4.41 *The center of Frank Lloyd Wright's Oak Park Studio.*

16) Orienting Entry

Definition

An orienting entry is a space or layer which establishes a clear understanding of the general nature and organization of the building and its activities.

Problem Statement

Wayfinding, an omnipresent criterion for Assisted Living, is particularly important at places of entry, where orientation to paths and desired destinations is of utmost importance.

ARCHITECTURAL DESIGN CONSIDERATIONS

Figure 4.42 *The entry hall of the Glessner House leads one into a central figural space with a powerful and memorable form and image.*

Discussion

The entry area in an assisted living residence is not only the place where residents and guests enter the facility and begin to understand the building's organization, but a very active social place as well, where staff and residents interact and need to be reoriented.

Design Consideration

Consider the entry space to be an enlarged vestibule, small hall, anteroom, or a series of layers adjacent to the main gathering space and primary horizontal and vertical circulation. The nature and ambiance of the building as a residence should be clear. (See Figure 4.42.) Relatively direct connection to the reception/observation area is an important safety consideration.

The place of entry could also provide places for people to sit, watch, and engage in the activity that normally occurs and draws attention and excitement at an entry.

A weighing of benefits of this accommodation depends on the level of cognitive impairment of residents and the philosophy regarding their care, as these residents may be encouraged by an active entry toward unwanted exits.

Rationale

The process of understanding a building in part involves the memory and relation of one space to the next. A clear relationship of an entry to the main stair and primary gathering space can provide meaningful and memorable cues to potential paths and places of activity.

At times, the activity happening at the entry may be interesting, as visitors, staff, family, and business people come and go. By providing a place or connection of places from which to casually observe entry activity, this natural desire is accommodated and normalized.

17) Continuous and Connecting Circulation Route

Definition

A continuous and connecting circulation is exterior and interior circulation that loops or forms an uninterrupted path.

Problem Statement

Discontinuous paths may confuse those with cognitive impairments who may arrive at a complicated crossing or dead end and become agitated or need intervention to reorient.

Discussion

For those with dementia or other cognitive impairments who may wander, paths that engage no activity or abruptly end may not only be the cause of confusion, but may deny these residents the potential for passive activity connections and spatial and behavioral orientation. In such conditions, the behavior of wandering can become an activity that is unpleasant for the resident. This can create an undignified and caregiver-dependent situation.

The lack of some enjoyable exterior or interior walking circuit denies the more able residents easy access to this pleasant and healthy activity.

Design Consideration

Circulation paths should be designed to form a continuous loop, connecting resident rooms with areas of activity and engagement along the path. Such an arrangement develops a circuit with interesting activity areas and places along it. (See Figure 4.43.)

Rationale

Looping or connecting circulation routes provide opportunities for enjoyable and accessible exercise, as well as meaningful wandering activity for those residents whose impairments may compel them to do so.

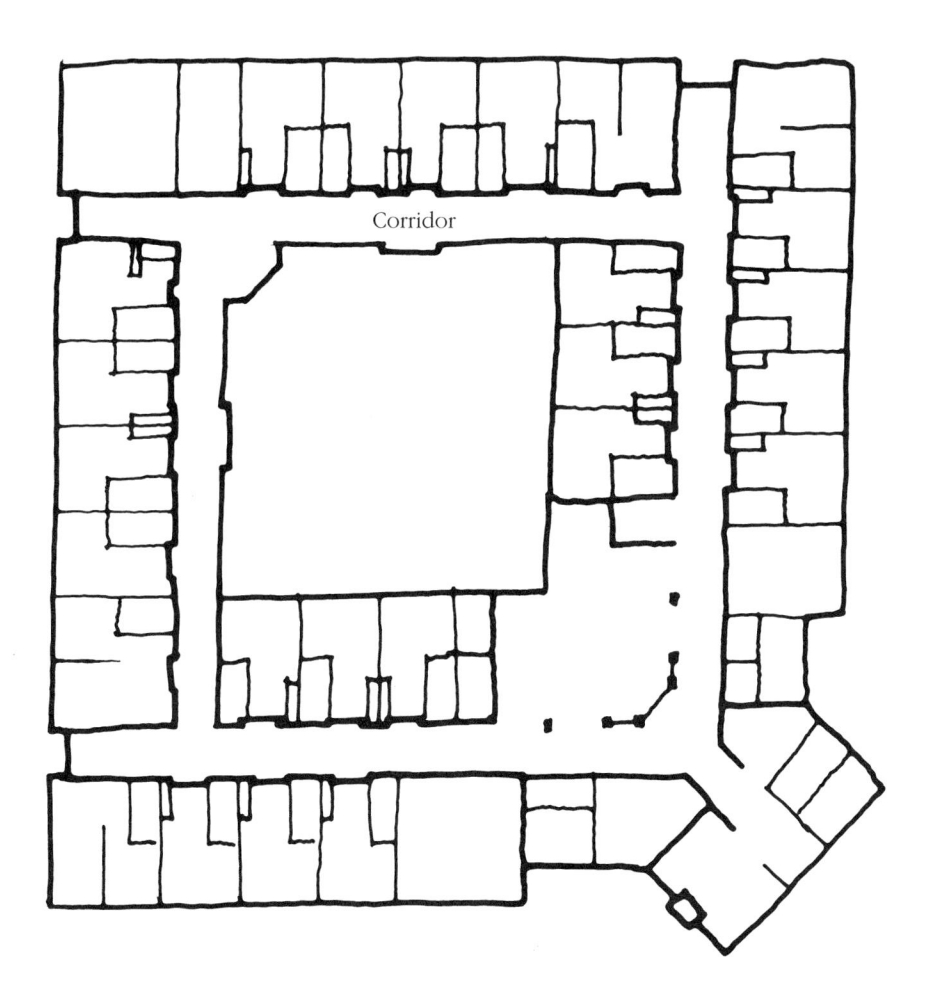

Figure 4.43 *(Below, left) The circumnavigating corridor at Rackleff House affords both meaningful wandering and enjoyable indoor strolling. (Chilles-Nielsen Architects.)*

QUALIFICATION

CONCEPT OF HOME: SECURITY/SAFETY

A place of shelter and safety.

CONCEPT OF HOME: CONTROL/AUTOTOMY

A place of control and freedom.

Supportive Architectural Characteristics of Home

a) The literal and visual movement from outside to inside takes place through a series of spaces or layers that describe the transition from the public domain to the private world. (See Figure 4.44.)

b) A private exterior realm is created, allowing for semiprivate outdoor activity. (See Figure 4.45.)

c) The home offers amenities and controls, which enable the owner to carry out a relatively independent and private lifestyle.

d) Home affords the owner the ability to control the environmental conditions within, such as light, temperature, ventilation, and opacity or transparency of its openings.

e) The home and the place/space amenities within it are closable and securable.

Discussion

The power to have reasonable control over one's own domain is fundamental to the concept of *home* (Norberg-Schultz, 1985). Control of inside-to-outside relationships, public-to-private participation in activity, general atmospheric conditions within, and control of the artifacts one keeps within, profoundly support these concepts.

Architectural Implications

The provision of a variety of kinds of space that are or can become relatively private and personal supports such freedoms. The ability of

Figure 4.44 *(Below, left) The porch at this coastal house by Steven Holl casts wonderful shadows, creating a veil-like layer between inside and out. (Berkowitz-Odgis House, Martha's Vineyard. Reproduced with permissions of Steven Holl Architects.)*

Figure 4.45 *(Below) Another Holl house discusses the notion of the importance and meaning of a defined private outdoor realm. (Van Zandt House, East Hampton. Reproduced with permission of Steven Holl Architects.)*

the occupant to manipulate visual and physical accessibility to the interior of the home is a subtle yet important consideration.

Comprehensive, fully usable and adaptable amenities within each apartment create a distinct and complete home, signifying that it is indeed a place accommodating the independent lifestyle of a capable individual.

18) Layered Building Envelope

Definition

A layered front or edge is one where the transition from inside to outside takes place as a sequence of spaces, events, or architectural elements.

Problem Statement

A hard street-building edge, one in which the private interior is separated from the public exterior by no transition space, is typically inconsistent with the notions of shelter and privacy.

Discussion

A building's initial reading from the street edge sets a conceptual context from which all other aspects of the building are discerned. Setbacks or front yard spaces that are incompatible with the existing residential pattern within the context could create an ambiguity with respect to the nature of the place, or produce an overly public or institutional misunderstanding of it by both visitors and residents.

The lack of any "in-between" space rejects supporting the casual and comfortable, passive and active connections that take place between the interior realm of the home and the outer world.

Figure 4.46 *Architect Herman Hertzberger designed a special seating space at this stairway landing, providing a light and airy interior resting spot where the building faces the street.*

Design Consideration

Consider designing a system of layered interior and exterior spaces at the place where the building meets the street. The design of special spaces such as porches, sunrooms, decks, greenhouses, and screened porches could be explored. Variety in the character, identity, size, solar orientation, and level of atmospheric separation from the outside could expand a building's richness. (See Figure 4.46.)

Patterns within the context that describe places as "home" from the street edge such as setbacks, front yard spaces, walks, or verandas, should be integrated into the design in order to support the place as a residence and cue appropriate, known, and expected behavior about it.

The exception to this guideline may be in relation to a commercial/public component within the facility, which may need to reach beyond this residential territorial realm to engage the public.

Rationale

Architectural elements such as these reinforce the understanding of the complex as a whole as being primarily private, and provide a clear transition from outside to in.

In addition, such spaces allow the more-frail residents some of the opportunity and experience of the outdoors and the street, while still controlling the effects of some of the potentially harmful natural elements (Gaskie, 1988).

19) Private Outdoor Space

Definition

Private outdoor space includes balconies, porches, decks, and other outdoor places which are directly connected, and private, to resident apartments.

Problem Statement

The exclusion of private outdoor space denies residents' ability and opportunity to choose from a full range of activity to engage in.

Figure 4.47 *A small private garden and secondary apartment entrance.*

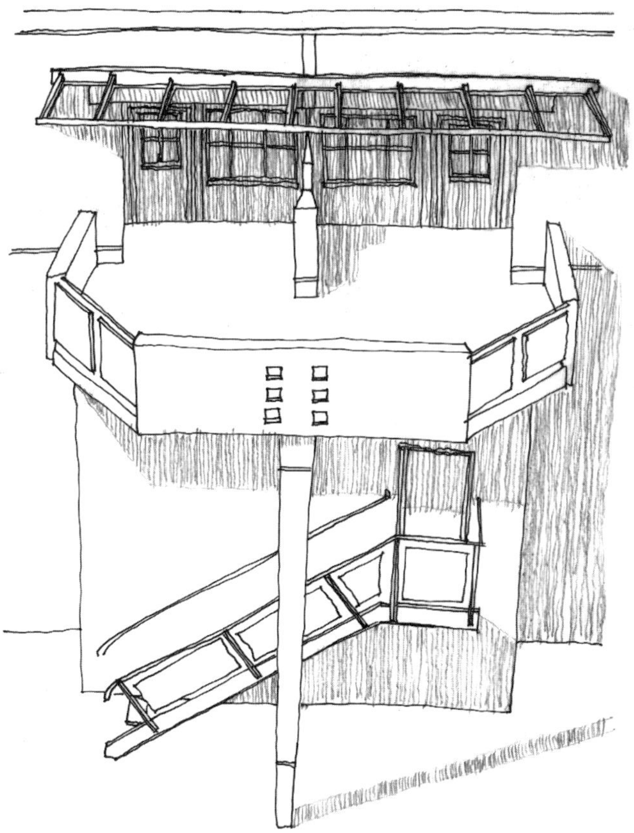

Figure 4.48 *This deck provides a setting for informal socialization.*

Discussion

The kind of informal activity of people watching and relaxing that may take place most comfortably in private outdoor space is deeply referential to normal homelike activity.

Independence is also supported by the affordance of outdoor space that is easily accessible from residents' apartments.

Another positive effect of providing such is its potential enhancement to the exterior facade of the building. Edge layers, such as porches and decks, contribute much to the character and scale of the building, and provide an opportunity to delineate individual units.

Design Consideration

Provide private outdoor space accessible from, and private to, each resident apartment. In a smaller facility, this space may become a small private patio or garden (see Figure 4.47), or a private edge onto a shared space. A private outdoor space may take the form of a balcony or deck in a multistory building. (See Figure 4.48.)

Rationale

Resident choice, control, and opportunities for privacy are extended by offering a space for private outdoor activity. A direct connection to the outdoors increases opportunities for orientation to time of day and year, weather conditions, and place/context (Regnier, 1994).

20) Useful Kitchenette

Definition

A *fully equipped* kitchen space or edge within resident apartments is a useful kitchenette.

Problem Statement

An important part of the identity of "home" is the place where meals are prepared and taken, and sustenance is kept, as well as the place where meals are offered (Rybczynski, 1986). Resident apartments that are not equipped to support such deny this fundamental aspect of home.

Discussion

Again, resident choice, independence, and autonomy are at the heart of this consideration. Many residents may not wish to, or be able to, use a kitchenette, yet the affordance of such has important symbolic value as well as literal worth.

A kitchenette may also be a place where a guest can prepare a meal for the resident and themselves in the privacy of the apartment.

For more-capable residents, the ability to choose what and when to have a meal or snack if they desire supports their independence and the notion of the place as home as defined by its *potential activity*.

Design Consideration

Include in the design of resident apartments a kitchenette complete with a sink, refrigerator, electric stove and oven, countertop, homelike casework, and task lighting shaded from residents' eyes. (See Figure 4.49.) This kitchenette should be accessible, or easily adaptable to residents using electric carts or wheelchairs. Special consider-

Figure 4.49 *A fully equipped and well-used kitchenette in a resident apartment.*

ation should be given to the ability to turn off, adapt, or remove the stove/oven, since this could become a hazard to those with advanced cognitive impairments.

Rationale

Some residents may wish to take a snack or light meal in privacy and comfort from time to time, make a pot of coffee in the morning before they are "presentable," or offer a guest something to eat or drink. Such opportunities connect their apartment with a place that operates and affords the behaviors, activities, aromas, and sounds of home.

21) PERSONALLY ADJUSTABLE APARTMENT CONTROLS

Definition

This consideration refers to a resident's ability to lock his/her own apartment as well as having control over the interior environmental control systems within their apartments.

Problem Statement

An inability to control one's own space could significantly undermine the important acknowledgment of a resident's apartment as personal, safe, secure, and personally adaptable space.

Discussion

A resident's sense of autonomy and independence is a key issue regarding this simple consideration. Fear or uneasiness regarding potentially unwanted and unexpected intrusion could eclipse one's comfort and inhibition level within one's own home.

Design Consideration

Provide locking apartment doors and individual apartment lighting and HVAC controls (i.e., a thermostat).

Senior staff could have access to master keys for intervention in case of an accident or emergency.

Special consideration and accommodation would have to be taken regarding those with critical and quickly changing health conditions, as well as those with advanced stages of cognitive impairments.

Rationale

Providing residents with their own environmental controls and lockable doors not only fosters their own sense of control, dignity, privacy, and autonomy, but supports their rights as capable and trustworthy individuals. Lockable doors also serve as a constantly available reassurance of personal safety as well as the security of one's belongings.

22) Easy Adaptability to Changing Needs

Definition

Easy adaptability refers to the ability for the physical environment to be reasonably manipulated and changed, even by those with physical and cognitive limitations.

Problem Statement

Assisted living facility residents' needs often change or develop over time, potentially requiring an adjustment or compensation in both procedure and environment.

Discussion

With a philosophy of aging in place, an Assisted Living environment that is unable to respond or adapt to the changes that may take place through aging, is only partially supportive of residents' needs over time. Such an inability to adapt, even at a myopic level, may force some residents, as their needs increase, to become more dependent on the caregiving staff, relocate to another apartment, or even move to a more intensive setting.

Design Consideration

At a macro scale, this could imply the ability of a shared room to easily adapt to a variety of activities, such as a living room that also serves as a place for group exercise, an activity kitchen that doubles as a craft area, or a resident's apartment that can be a comfortable living space for one person or a couple. (See Figure 4.50.)

At a micro scale, this could mean the ability of a resident's apartment to easily adapt for a owner in a wheelchair, an apartment entry alcove that can also be used for parking and recharging electric wheelchairs/carts, or doors that can be opened or omitted in an apartment bathroom to provide quick and easy access for a resident with cognitive impairments or incontinence.

Figure 4.50 *An alcove, typically intended as a sleeping space in this facility, is transformed by the resident into a dining space.*

Rationale

An environment specifically designed to respond to residents' changing needs supports issues of permanence, consistency, and independence (AARP, 1993). Anticipation of the necessity to enable small-scale adaptability increases stay longevity and hence is responsive to these issues. By providing opportunities and affordances for such changes to take place relatively easily, the experience of having to make a change in response to changing needs becomes less traumatic, normalized, and may be initiated by the resident themselves.

23) Ample and Unemcumbered Spaces with Support

Definition

This guideline refers to the design of spaces large enough and with appropriate physical support to enable frail or impaired residents to perform desired activities.

Problem Statement

Many residents of assisted living facilities may have mobility impairments or other frailties that could make it difficult for them to access places, features, furniture, or activities.

Discussion

Residents often enter an assisted living facility in part because their independent home involves obstacles to access, and provides little physical support in terms of accommodations for disabilities. If residents are impeded from access to or participation in an activity or event because of difficulties or obstacles in the physical environment, a loss of independence and choice may result.

Design Consideration

Ensure that all spaces and elements are wheelchair, electric scooter, and walker accessible. Consider the potentially limited strength, dexterity, coordination, and mobility of a frail resident. Explore the adaptation of normal, homelike elements, such as a chair rail or wainscot trim that is widened to provide a handrail or edge to lean against along corridors and public spaces in lieu of an institutional grab bar. (See Figure 4.51.)

Bathrooms should have appropriate construction, fixtures, and wall backing to allow for easy adaptation for a frail or mobility-impaired resident. (See Figure 4.52.)

Consideration of an electric outlet for wheelchair recharging in an accessible yet nonencumbering way should be taken.

Rationale

The philosophy of Assisted Living considers residents' ability to remain in the facility (as opposed to being discharged to a more

Figure 4.51 *(Above, left) A chair rail, integrated into the corridor window design, unobtrusively provides support.*

Figure 4.52 *(Above, Right) An accessible bathroom which maintains its residential character.*

24) Responsive Elements and Hardware

intensive setting as conditions deteriorate) paramount (Wilson, 1993). With potential mobility impairments and the likelihood of a decrease in abilities over time, a very large portion of assisted living residence residents can be accommodated by giving this issue its due attention.

Definition

Responsive elements and hardware are relatively independently usable by most residents, even those with physical and cognitive impairments.

Problem Statement

Assisted living residents with physical or cognitive impairments may find complex or strenuous tasks and manipulations difficult or confusing.

Discussion

Many residents have or may develop limitations with regard to flexibility, dexterity, strength, and range of motion as a result of arthritis, stroke, or other debilitating condition. Those with Alzheimer's disease or similar conditions may find tasks or manipulations requiring new knowledge or multiple or coordinated movements relatively incomprehensible (Hodkinson, 1988)

Design Consideration

Specify throughout lever hardware that is easily manipulated and requires lower-than-normal force to operate. Casework, shelving, and kitchen and bathroom fixtures should be placed in locations considerate of residents' reduced ability to reach high and stoop low, and their typically lower center of gravity and eye level. (See Figure 4.53.)

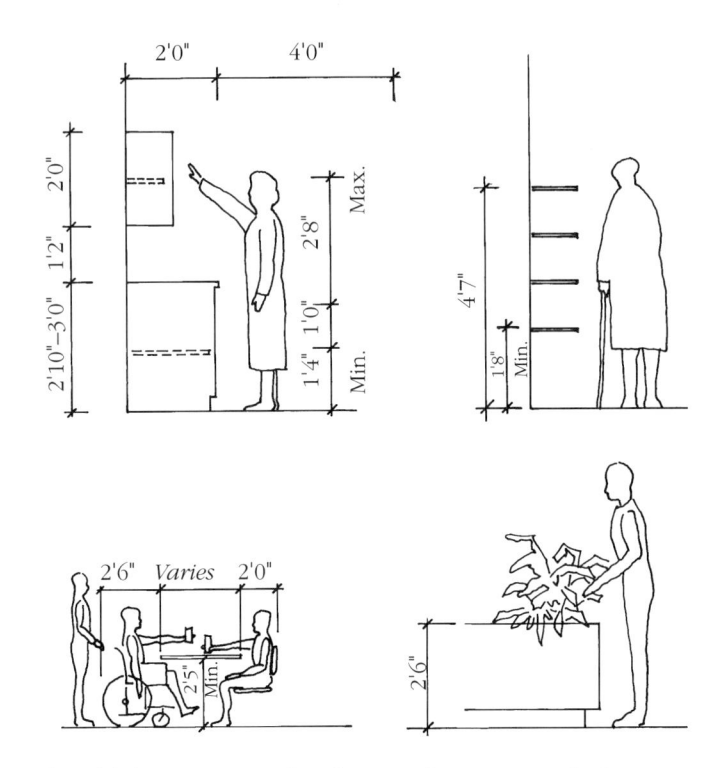

Figure 4.53 (Left) *Dimensional guidelines considering people with limited strength, mobility, dexterity, and reach.*

Figure 4.54 (Above, right) *A door handle with powerful and memorable tactile and visual qualities in a Frank Israel-designed house.*

Consideration should be given to hardware, fixtures, and elements that meet these demands, yet avoid highly institutional images, applications, or textures.

Opportunity exists in the specification of hardware to reinforce desired orientation, activity cueing, and place identity. An item such as a door lever that is frequently touched could carry special tactile and visual qualities that provide such cues. (See Figure 4.54.)

Rationale

The ability of frail and impaired residents to easily access spaces and elements affords opportunities for independently accessing and performing tasks, thereby supporting resident autonomy, control, dignity, and independence. The Assisted Living environment should be one in which many of the physical obstacles and difficulties to living and operating independently are eliminated. In addition, increased ability for residents to act independently lessons the burden on the caregiving staff.

25) PUSH, PULL, TEST, AND REINTERPRET RESTRICTIONS AND REGULATIONS

Definition

This consideration refers to the roles of the designer, developer, contractor, and owner in challenging antiquated codes and restrictions.

Problem Statement

In most jurisdictions, Assisted Living as a building type or social phenomena is not clearly identified nor defined, and has no distinct or appropriate set of regulations.

Discussion

As a new and evolving building and service type, Assisted Living often falls between codified definitions that outline building, safety, and health requirements and standards. Officials must then make judgments regarding which set of existing regulations should apply (often on a project-by-project basis). These judgments may sometimes be founded on a lack of knowledge or understanding regarding the nature and intent of Assisted Living, and are often derived through overly conservative and antiquated paradigms.

Design Consideration

Challenge codes, regulations, and restrictions that are inappropriate, overly protective, or otherwise are offspring of the hospital/institutional model of care.

Search for new and creative solutions to questions of material, construction, procedures, and equipment that are safe and reasonable yet do not compromise the integrity of the home environment. This may involve a negotiated level of risk, or a compromise between durability and character.

In some instances, this may also involve diplomatic education regarding the nature of an assisted living residence and its residents.

Rationale

One of the greatest threats to continued evolution of the better models of Assisted Living is inappropriate regulation. Debilitating regulation is certainly one significant reason for the lack of quality or character in typical nursing home environments. As creators of a new building type, building and health care professionals, as well as owners, must become advocates for appropriate regulations by challenging inappropriate ones.

26) Unobtrusive Reception/Observation

Definition

A caregiver reception and observation area is a place where staff members can receive and direct visitors, guests, and residents and, in general, oversee the activities within the facility, while performing daily tasks. An unobtrusive reception area is informal and does not interrupt the domestic identity of the facility.

Problem Statement

The pragmatic need for the reception area to be relatively centrally located (to limit staff travel distances and maximize oversight) can often lead to placing it in an obtrusively central and visually dominating location. This can serve as a constant implication to visitors and residents that residents are being "cared for" and under "supervision."

Discussion

Few single architectural features could more profoundly undermine residents' associations of the facility with home or their feelings of independence, autonomy, and dignity than the presence of an imposing institution-like nurse station. A dominating observation space suggests institutional procedure and control (Kane, 1990). Competing notions of the place as "one's home"—a place under one's territory and control—and a "nurse's ward"—a place where staff initiate actions and control events—will likely arise. Furthermore, the ambiance of this area may present confusion or ambiguity with respect to the nature of the building as home.

Design Consideration

Create a reception area that reinforces the homelike character and quality of the facility. One approach to doing so is locating this area to the *edge* of the central space, within view and access of the entry, main space, and circulation paths to resident rooms. In addition to placement, the character of this area should be aligned with the character of home. By translating the reception area into a den or kitchenlike area (see Figures 4.55, 4.56), using typical wooden casework, desks and shelves in lieu of high countertops and steel casework, and incandescent task lighting in lieu of fluorescence, this character can be achieved.

Rationale

By adapting this space in such manners, the potential negative impact of the necessary reception area is minimized. Such character can also serve to influence and remind the staff of the nature of the place and their role in relating to it and the residents.

Figure 4.55 *A desk acts as a normalized reception counter at Sunrise Retirement Home of Arlington.*

Figure 4.56 *A reception/observation and staff work area in Woodside Place is designed as a kitchenlike space—unobtrusive yet very useful and accommodating for staff.*

27) Normalized and Positive Bathing

Definition

A bathing room for occasional staff assistance in resident hygiene is necessary in an assisted living residence. A normalized and positive bathing experience approximates the casualness, comfort, enjoyment, and privacy of bathing at home.

Problem Statement

The normal boundaries of privacy and dignity are at risk when one must gain assistance in an activity as traditionally private as bathing. Traditional environmental and equipment solutions to safe bathing for those who need assistance often ignore the potential psychological traumas they may induce as abnormal, awkward, frightening, and undignified machines.

Since the room itself may be used by more than one resident on any given day, the need to avoid embarrassing or inappropriate interruptions is an important concern.

Discussion

Maximizing resident dignity, privacy, and control is of critical issue in an activity such as assisted bathing. This is in part a factor of how accessible and potentially independently operable the bathing room and apparatus are, and partially a matter of how the bathing room is designed and operated considering residents' privacy.

Design Consideration

Design the bathing room in a manner that provides shielding between the door into the room and the bath and area directly in front of the bath. A small vestibule between bathing room entry door and the bath with curtains to pull shut when the room is in use, serves as a clear visual cue that suggests to those who may enter that the room is in use.

Consider the specification of accessible bathing appliances that allow residents to access the tub relatively easily from the side from a wheelchair or walker, without having to be lifted by staff or awkward machine in order to enter. (See Figure 4.57.) Flooring should be nonslip, and wall and floor finishes should be water resistant yet with a character consistent with home. Easily movable curtains, valances, etc., could be employed to help disguise an unusual tub, and wood casework, shelving, and furniture should also be considered. Incandescent lighting that is adjustable could be turned up to a bright level for careful bathing and condition check, and then dimmed to allow a resident to "steal" a relaxing moment.

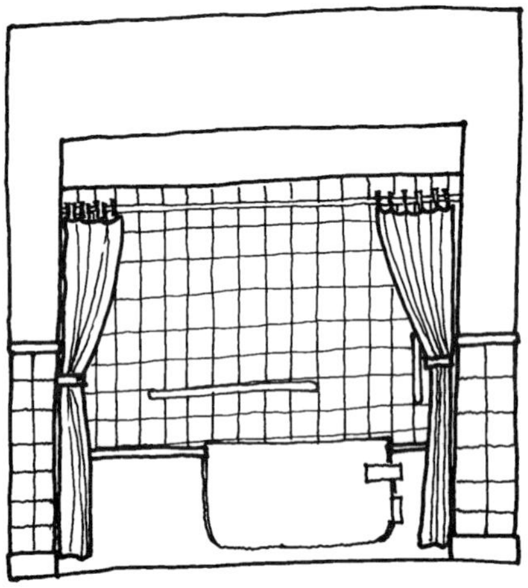

Rationale

Providing a bathing appliance and room design for maximum potential for residents to bathe relatively independently, or at least

Figure 4.57 *A nonobtrusive side-entry bathtub.*

86   THE ESSENCE OF HOME

take a primary role in the activity, embraces the privacy and dignity issues. By creating homelike character within the bathing room and maximizing opportunities for positive experience during bathing, this unusual and potentially undignified and traumatic experience could be tempered.

Concept of Home: Choice/Opportunity

A place of chosen opportunities, activities, and lifestyle; a place for challenge and stimulation.

Supportive Architectural Characteristics of Home

a) The home is designed considering rooms and spaces that serve specific purposes to daily life. (See Figure 4.58.)

b) Casual visual connections are possible from one (nonprivate) realm to another, affording opportunity to choose entrance and participation or passive observation. (See Figure 4.59.)

c) The home accommodates visitors by providing space for entertainment, and some accommodation can be made for overnight visitors. A kitchen allows a host to offer something to a guest.

Discussion

Generic, nondescript, and visually separated "activity rooms" offer little in terms of architectural cues as to their purpose or possible use. No home includes such lifeless, uninspiring places, and providing such only stirs institutional connotations.

Purposeful spaces inspired by the uses, activities, and comforts of home do not necessarily limit the activity possibilities that can occur within. Rather, they cue a range of meaningful and comfortable engagements.

Figure 4.58 *(Below, left) H.H. Richardson's Glessner House library.*

Figure 4.59 *(Below, right) Visual connection is afforded from the private to the more public area of the Weingarten Residence by Ace Architects through this central open space.*

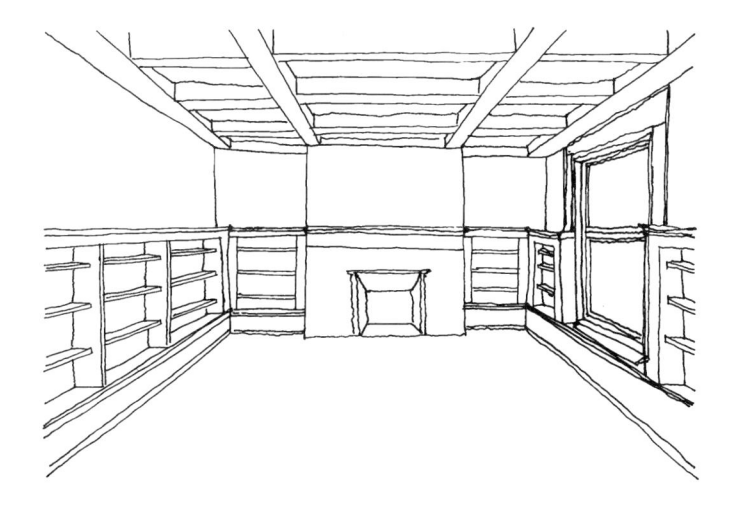

Architectural Implications

Consider a variety of specific activities that relate to normal, daily life when designing rooms and shared spaces. Themes can be drawn from home life to enrich the design development of shared spaces.

28) PURPOSEFUL EXTERIOR ROOMS

Definition

Purposeful exterior rooms are designed with specific and potential activities and uses in mind, and may be in the back or front of the building.

Problem Statement

Physical environments that are unspecific and unclaimed are generally unused, uninspiring, cue little activity, and are often misunderstood as institutional (Cooper-Marcus, 1986).

Discussion

Ambiguous, leftover exterior space is typically inconsistent with the pattern of most homes, where private yards are traditionally prized. Undefined exterior space represents a missed opportunity to provide a space for activities and events supporting engaging, enjoyable, and therapeutic experience outdoors.

Design Consideration

Develop exterior realms which relate to normal, homelike activities and experiences. Themes developed could include gardens with raised planting beds of vegetables or flowers (see Figure 4.60); a pavilion-centered or arcade-edged courtyard (see Figure 4.61); a workshop-centered backyard with light tools for carpentry and crafts; a greenhouse yard for winter gardening; or a deck with a series of umbrellaed tables. In dense urban sites, an interior atrium or courtyard may provide exteriorlike qualities and orientations. (See Figure 4.62.)

Figure 4.60 (Below, left) Raised planting beds afford accessible gardening.

Figure 4.61 (Below, right) A pavilion-centered courtyard at Regency Park, Portland, Oregon.

Figure 4.62 *A fountain-centered courtyard.*

Rationale

The creation of purposeful outdoor places provides opportunities for residents to partake in familiar and therapeutic activity that stimulates the mind and body. Outdoor activity, particularly activities such as planting and tending a garden, help to orient residents to time of day and year, and provide opportunities for socialization and purposeful experience.

29) CENTRAL DINING WITH INTIMATE SCALE

Definition

A central dining room refers to a resident-shared dining space where staff-prepared meals can be taken by residents. Intimate scale refers to a dining ambiance that supports smaller social groups and tables of residents within the larger dining space.

Problem Statement

The pragmatic operational need to create a relatively central dining space for larger groups of residents (or the entire resident population) to take meals can result in a dining environment that is of a large scale, inconsistent with home and distracting to the enjoyment and focus of taking a meal with friends.

Discussion

The advantage of a relatively central dining space is not one of efficiency only. Dining itself can be a highly enjoyable and orienting experience. The ability of this activity to potentially become a major focus or experiential heart of the facility can support many of the activities and behaviors most closely associated with home. Some residents may take on a meaningful role in the meal preparation, table

ARCHITECTURAL DESIGN CONSIDERATIONS 89

setting, seating, or clearing routine. Others may simply enjoy casually watching this activity in anticipation of their meal. The multisensory stimulation and cueing potentials of the sounds of preparation and the aromas of food further suggest a relatively central dining experience.

A large, undifferentiated dining space, however, may produce high levels of ambient noise and activity during serving, eating, and clearing that may be particularly distracting or confusing, especially for those with cognitive impairments. This may limit attention spans or ability to focus on tasks or the activities of eating and conversation (Cohen and Weisman, 1991).

Design Consideration

Locate dining rooms in a manner that is experientially central, connecting this fundamentally homelike and social experience with the heart of the facility. This may or may not, however, place the dining room in the physical center. The appropriateness of the placement depends largely on the size of the facility, its organizational order, and the nature and abundance of its other shared spaces. The intent is that through placement and connectedness, the dining room and its activity presents a clear, orienting, and immediate experience. (See Figure 4.63.)

The character and scale of the dining room should be considered to promote a comfortable and homelike sharing of meals. Features such as bays and alcoves, private dining rooms adjoining the main dining room, a fireplace, and intimate tables for four to eight people, support possibilities for a more intimate and pleasant dining experience. (See Figure 4.64.)

Depending on the size of the facility, the organizational strategy of the apartments, and the nature of the residents, dining may happen in one larger dining room or a series of shared dining rooms for clusters or groups of residents.

Toilet rooms should be located near dining rooms in a clear manner.

Figure 4.63 *(Below, left) The dining room at the Glessner house is a central bay extending into the courtyard—a dominant space viewed along the main circulation route and across the courtyard as a figural element.*

Figure 4.64 *(Below, right) The dining room at Rosewood at Roseville is designed to provide more intimate alcoves and subspaces near windows and a fireplace.*

Rationale

The activities, aromas, tastes, and sounds of dining and the preparation for it compose a complete multisensory event that encourages socialization, paces and orients the day, provides opportunities for caregiving staff to maintain important connections with all of the residents, and is fundamental to the experience of home (Regnier, 1991).

Access and orientation to nearby toilet rooms supports independent maintenance for residents who may struggle with incontinence (Kalymun, 1993).

30) Casual Preview

Definition

A casual preview is a space, layer, or edge area where the activity of another space can be unobtrusively viewed by someone from another space prior to entering it.

Problem Statement

In a group living situation, personal preference in terms of activity and socialization may vary greatly. Entering a space with an undesired activity or group event taking place may cause uncomfortable and unhealthy stress and tension.

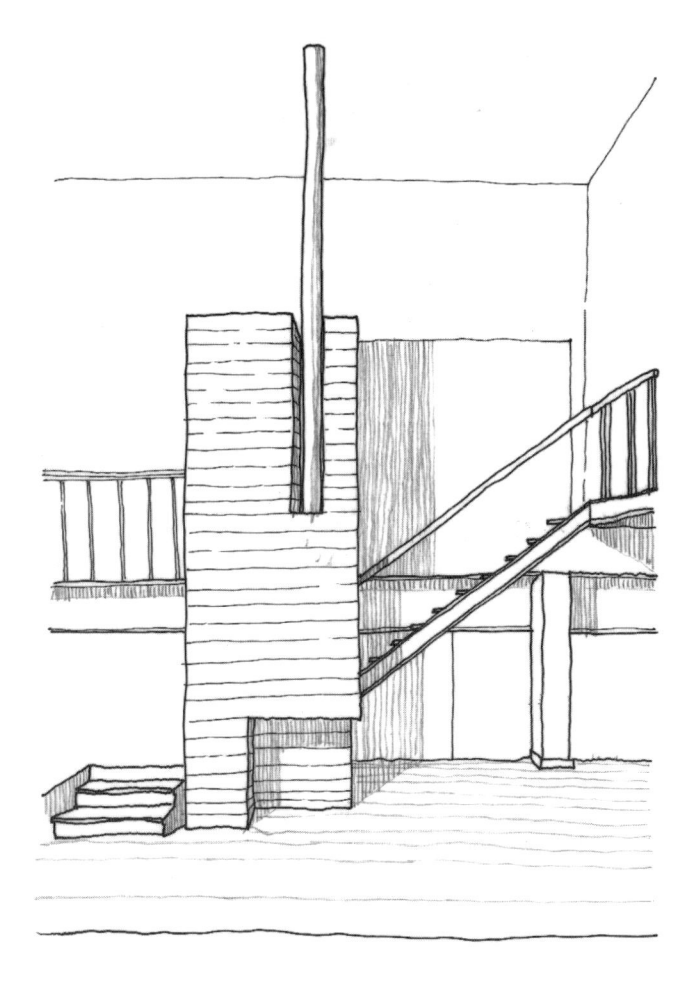

Figure 4.65 *The staircase in this residence by Roto Architects acts as a central orienting and previewing object.*

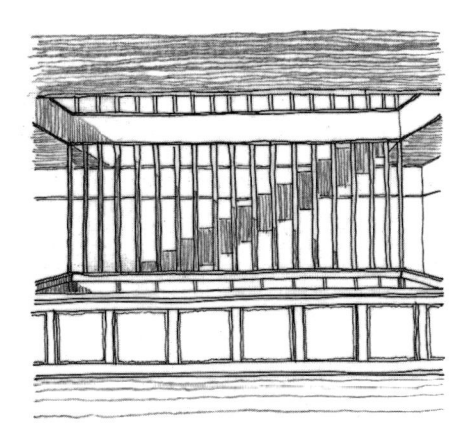

Figure 4.66 *Preview is afforded through this staircase screen wall in the Charnley House by Louis Sullivan.*

Discussion

The inability to ascertain the nature of the activity and occupants in a shared space can potentially lead to inappropriate or unwanted entering or participation of an event or activity. Concern about such, and the inability to understand the situation and unobtrusively make a comfortable decision, may cause some residents to avoid unknown or unplanned activities.

Previewing of a space and the activity in it prior to entering it, from a position where the resident has the ability to make a decision whether or not to enter the space, clarifies the order by making more of it visible and understandable, and allows the resident to make a casual and informed decision about the activities and environments they wish to experience.

Design Consideration

Design casual previews to active spaces. This can be arranged through alignment of interior openings or voids from one space to another (see Figure 4.65), or the use of layers, edges, or platforms between one space and another. (See Figure 4.66.)

Rationale

By providing the opportunity for residents to preview and make informed decisions, resident autonomy and choice is supported in a manner that avoids uncomfortable decision-making or social situations. In addition, previews may alleviate some of the potential tensions of group living, by reducing the number of uncomfortable and unwanted situations.

Preview spaces and layers also provide settings for comfortable, passive participation, and people and activity watching (Regnier, 1994).

31) Eventful and Enjoyable Stairway

Definition

This consideration refers to open stairways that are an important event within the facility, and which overlook and connect to a main activity space.

Problem Statement

In a multistory building, vertical disorientation may create a problem, particularly for those with cognitive and sensory impairments.

Discussion

The experience of riding in an elevator or ascending an enclosed stairway can be disorienting. One may not have a clear understanding of which floor one is on or which floor particular activity spaces are located.

The lack of an element/space which *links and orients* a multi-story facility *vertically* denies both the sectional understanding of the place and the opportunity for preview to happen vertically as well as horizontally.

Design Consideration

Design open stairways that edge, overlook, and become part of the main shared space. These can provide an important orienting, vertical link, and spatial and experiential variety and hierarchy. Beautiful, elegant, and finely detailed staircases can become such elements that recall the richness of Victorian or Bungalow homes. (See Figure 4.67).

Rationale

An open stairway with a vertical space that links upstairs and downstairs can become an important reorienting and centering device (Hoglund, 1989). Even if a resident cannot physically climb the stairway, the visual cue it provides reveals and restates the order of the place.

In addition, an enjoyable and eventful stairway encourages resident use, promoting some daily exercise.

Figure 4.67 *Ascending and descending are an event along the elegantly detailed main stairs of the Madeline House, Chicago.*

32) Places for Enjoyable Rest

Definition

Places for rest are small, out-of-the-way spaces along the main horizontal and vertical circulation routes. These spaces may be considered circulation eddy spaces just off the path.

Problem Statement

Some of the more frail or mobility-impaired residents of assisted living residences may find it difficult to traverse longer distances or vertical ascents or descents without a rest.

Discussion

Mobility impairments, arthritic, respiratory, and/or coronary conditions may make walking a difficult, tiring, and even painful experience for some assisted living residence residents. Having no place to rest along circulation routes may urge frail residents to mobilize with assistance, since they are unable to traverse the longer distance alone. This can potentially have a negative impact on residents' sense of independence, dignity, and choice, as possibilities become limited by their necessary travel distance.

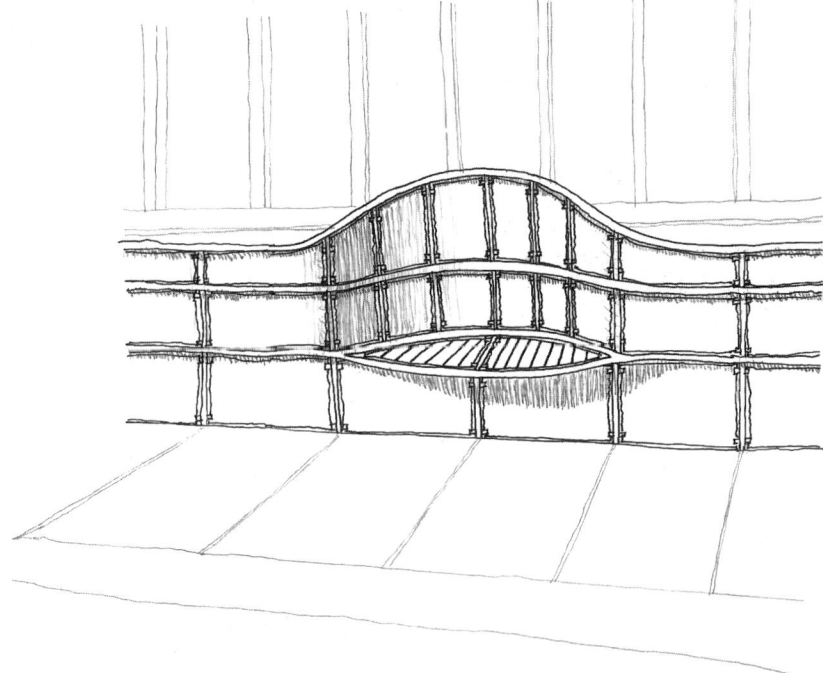

Figure 4.68 (Above, left) A sitting alcove with courtyard views along the single-loaded portion of the Rackleff House corridor.

Figure 4.69 (Above, right) A handrail gracefully becomes a sitting spot in a Herman Hertzberger building.

Design Consideration

Design alcoves, edges and transition spaces, and corridor-intervening spaces to provide places for needed rest and relaxation along horizontal and vertical circulation routes. These may also help to further deconstruct long or uneventful corridors. (See Figure 4.68.) Stair landings should occur frequently and be wide enough to accommodate benches or seats for residents to sit, rest, and overlook. (See Figure 4.69.)

Rationale

Providing enjoyable places for residents to rest along circulation routes considers conditions of frailty and immobility. Such spaces also make resting a pleasurable and expected occurrence, and provide potentially interesting, active, and orienting spaces along circulation routes.

33) LIVING ROOM ACTIVITY SPACES

Definition

Living room activity spaces refer to the relatively larger shared spaces within assisted living facilities that support casual, informal, and planned group activities, as well as provide living and social space for residents outside of their apartments.

Problem Statement

The problem often encountered when considering the design of the larger shared spaces is one of identity versus presumed flexibility. It is often assumed, particularly in institutional settings, that if a space is to be flexible in order to accommodate a variety of activities, it must be generic, with no particular identity and suggesting no manner of occupying or embracing the space.

Discussion

This "generic activity room" condition results in a space that cues or truly supports little activity (except to the staff who must work very hard to plan activity in it) and is entirely inconsistent with a home environment.

Relating the notion of "flexible" to "generic" often results in spaces that are void of architectural richness. Not only does the space have no identity but it has no beauty, either.

Design Consideration

Develop the main gathering space and the larger, more-active spaces with themes drawn from home, such as living room, parlor, sunroom, screened porch, card room, or billiard room. Avoid the generic "activity room," adaptable to any activity (but specific to, and implicative of, none). These rooms should include typical elements, character, and furnishings as those rooms in a home. (See Figures 4.70, 4.71.) These rooms should be large enough and somewhat adaptable to accommodate a variety of activities, and should be adjacent to the main circulation route. Consider layered transition spaces that provide opportunities for more passive participation as well as group and active engagement along the room's edge. Consideration of proximity to toilet rooms is also an important issue for those with incontinence.

Figure 4.70 *(Above, left) The powerful fireplace in the living room of the Croffead House by Clark and Menefee focuses the room with a purpose and a memorable icon. Upper floor rooms overlook this space, creating an active experiential center to the house.*

Figure 4.71 *(Above, right) The Sunroom at Roseville.*

ARCHITECTURAL DESIGN CONSIDERATIONS 95

Rationale

Rooms developed with homelike themes constitute places and elements of stability, familiarity, and consistency with past environments, supporting resident imaging and acceptance of the facility as home. Purposeful and familiar room identities prompt and cue activity possibilities, such as reading or visiting by the fireplace, watching movies or television, performing crafts or hobbies, exercising, or writing.

34) Small and Comfortable Shared Spaces

Definition

These spaces include the smaller, shared spaces in assisted living facilities that provide settings outside of residents' apartments for quieter, more focused, and intimate engagement.

Problem Statement

The need to provide these spaces which are common and shared, yet of a more intimate scale and identity, may be overlooked or underestimated in efforts to afford larger, more "universal" spaces.

Discussion

Such smaller-scaled spaces support a variety of environments in which to engage and socialize where smaller groups of residents and guests interact, quieter activity happens, focused groups participate in special activity, or residents who may be overwhelmed or agitated in larger settings can engage in calmer atmospheres.

The intention to consider purposeful design of these spaces, rich in character and homelike ambiance, corresponds to the discussion of the larger living room spaces.

Figure 4.72 *(Below, left) The Library at Annie Maxim House creates a setting for quiet activity and reflection.*

Figure 4.73 *(Below, right) The Pool Parlor at Mercer Island invites casual activity.*

Design Consideration

Along with the larger or more active shared spaces, consider intimate, casual, and comfortable shared spaces with corresponding themes drawn from home. These may include a library, den, study, drawing room, or breakfast nook. (See Figures 4.72, 4.73.) These rooms may be adjacent to the main circulation route, adjacent to larger, more active spaces, and/or dispersed throughout the building to provide small alcoves at locations along the circulation route.

Rationale

The provision of smaller and more passive shared spaces provides increased opportunities for resident choice and control regarding the nature of activity and experience (Pastalan, 1993).

35) Engaging Activity Kitchen

Definition

An activity kitchen is a resident-and staff-shared space, used as a setting for group cooking, baking, and perhaps craft activity.

Problem Statement

The activities involved in cooking, baking, and cleaning provide residents with potential connections to normal, familiar, and homelike tasks. Many residents, however, may be unable or unwilling to perform these activities completely independently in their own kitchenette in their apartment. The staff kitchen, and its more intensive activities, may well be an inappropriate setting for most residents.

Discussion

The issue of an activity kitchen relates both to environments that are supportive of residents' choice and control, and settings that offer therapeutic and social opportunities. A group-shared kitchen setting establishes a stage for meaningful activity and exchange, and provides a nonstigmatized environment for those who cannot cook or bake independently to enjoy the activity.

Design Consideration

Consider developing a useful and therapeutic activity kitchen, designed and equipped in a similar manner as a kitchen in a home. This kitchen should be located as an important activity node or edge, adjacent and visually connected to the dining room or main gathering space, and the main circulation route. (See Figure 4.74.)

This space should be finished with homelike yet washable floor and wall surfaces. Access by frail and mobility-impaired residents should be considered, including wheelchair-accessible spaces and

Figure 4.74 *The Activity Kitchen at Mercer Island adjoins the main corridor and a primary activity room, connecting strongly to the heart of the place and inviting participation.*

appliances, and a working surface at which residents could sit and perform tasks. Opportunity exists for this space to double as a useful and informal arts and crafts area or breakfast nook for smaller gatherings.

Rationale

The therapeutic benefits of affording and engaging residents (and potentially friends and family) in familiar, homelike tasks, such as cooking and baking include stimulation and challenge, ability maintenance and enhancing, casual opportunities for socialization, connections to fond and rewarding memories, and an increased sense of productivity, value, and belonging (Cohen and Weisman, 1991). In addition, the sights, sounds and aromas of cooking and baking are consistent with, and reinforce the identity of, the place as home.

36) Laundry as a Multisensory Experience

Definition

Considering laundering as a multisensory experience refers to the sensory stimulation and cues that the task of laundering provides.

Problem Statement

General laundering of linens, bedding, and other heavy-duty items is a task most assisted living facility residents are unable or unwilling to do. Yet, many consider the laundering of their clothes and personal items a matter of privacy and special care, and prefer to launder these items themselves. This creates the need for resident-accessible laundry facilities.

Discussion

The ability to have control over one's own personal items, and maintain one's personal laundry as a private matter retains residents' dignity and privacy. Laundering is also an activity which can be rich in homelike associations and memories, and provides an opportunity for residents to undertake and complete meaningful and worthwhile tasks.

Design Consideration

Develop the resident laundry room as a casual activity area along the circulation route, either adjacent to other shared spaces or as a special area along the path. (See Figure 4.75.)

If staff and residents share the same laundry space, it should be located near the reception/observation area for easy staff access while doing other tasks.

Distance from residents' rooms to the laundry room should be minimized as much as possible. Consideration for frail or mobility-impaired residents is important, and may include accessible appli-

Figure 4.75 *The resident- and staff-shared Laundry Room at Annie Maxim House is located directly off of the corridor, relatively central to the building, and enclosed with windowed walls, providing views into it.*

ances and storage shelves, an ironing board that easily folds down from a wall, and laundry folding table which can accommodate sitting while folding laundry.

Rationale

The opportunity for residents to do their own laundering supports their independence as capable persons. The task of doing laundry is a familiar household chore, full of the scents and sounds of churning washers and dryers that comprise sensory cues that reinforce the nature of the place as home.

37) Adaptive Office Connection

Definition

An adaptive office connection refers to the ability of the work/office space to support the potential for a variety of levels of quiet and uninterrupted work *and* observation and interaction.

Problem Statement

Staffing regimes may vary considerably in assisted living residences from day to night and with changing populations. At some times, a caregiver who is performing paperwork or other duties may also need to observe the facility, while at other times, they may require noninterrupted quiet.

Discussion

A delineation between quieter staff areas and the whole of the facility that is flexible from relatively open to closed supports opportunities for residents to socialize with staff when appropriate, and also allows staff the opportunity to focus and maintain privacy and concentration.

Design Consideration

Locate and design the separation of the staff office in a manner that allows for a variety of levels of staff-resident interaction and private and productive work. This could be accomplished by locating the office adjacent to the staff reception area and near the main entrance, circulation route, or an activity space. The separation between the two realms could be a wall with interior windows and curtains, a thoughtfully located door with a window and curtain, or an opening in the separating wall with wooden shutters. Lighting, finishes, and furnishings, which reinforce a homelike image, should be integrated. (See Figure 4.76.)

Rationale

The extent to which the administrating staff interact with residents and accommodate them in their office space depends largely on the

Figure 4.76 *Dutch doors are used at Woodside Place of Oakmont, Pennsylvania as a means of easily adapting privacy levels between a resident's room and the corridor. Such an approach could be applied at staff office areas, accommodating ease of privacy control.*

scale of the facility, the philosophy of care, and the importance of the tasks of the day. The ability to adjust this level of interaction takes into account the varying degrees of privacy that may be desired. The adjustment of these elements by staff can provide clear cues as to the privacy desired or interaction welcomed.

CHAPTER 5

BEHAVIORAL CONSIDERATIONS

INTRODUCTION

Since the concepts of home involve a complex interaction of behavior and environment, it is important to consider both aspects when attempting to create homelike character. Therefore, this section will outline behavioral philosophies, approaches, and strategies for integrating homelike character with Assisted Living.

This chapter is intended to be a *brief overview,* providing a basic understanding of the behavioral aspects and issues in order to further inform the designer of the desired nature of activity and behavior to be supported by the environment. This chapter in no way represents a comprehensive text on the complex subject of the behavioral, operational, and procedural dimensions of Assisted Living. (See the Bibliography for further reference regarding this subject matter.) It should also be noted that this work does not specifically address the very special needs of those with more advanced stages of Alzheimer's disease or similar conditions. Many times, those with such advanced conditions may require care and programming beyond the range or capability of a typical assisted living residence.

PHILOSOPHIES/APPROACHES

Assisted Living is considered a service-rich environment (Kalymun, 1991). This section describes service delivery in terms of behavioral/procedural response to resident needs.

Integrative philosophies and approaches to responding to these needs will be discussed in terms of activities of daily living, social enrichment, and psychological well-being. Then, strategies concerning these behavioral aspects will be drawn that attempt to reconcile the concepts and services of Assisted Living with the principles of home, and mitigate the potential contradictions.

1) Activities of Daily Living

Philosophy/Approach: Ability-Enhancing versus Caregiving

The majority of needed assistance and services in an assisted living residence relate to residents' normal activities of daily living such as dressing, grooming, toileting, bathing, meal preparation and eating, and getting from place to place. An approach that considers the facility the residents' household implies relationships between staff and residents centering on respecting residents' privacy, dignity, autonomy, and independence.

An assistance environment that embraces residents' abilities and their need to maintain and expand those abilities shifts the focus from caregiving to ability-enhancing.

Assistance given as needed as opposed to as scheduled (Kalymun, 1991), and according to changing needs, maintains a personalized, individualized manner of care, fostering residents' images of unique self.

Shared responsibility for well-being between staff and residents allows the resident to be an integral part of choosing his or her level and type of assistance, including the choice to assume reasonable risk, and again maintains the resident's sense of control and autonomy over his/her environment.

Some assistance could be the source of personal embarrassment, and many assistance activities are private matters. Utmost respect for residents' dignity and privacy must be maintained.

Regulations that empower the resident and the resident's family with the ability to choose needed services or assume reasonable risk and remain in assisted living residences, by adapting the environment and service level, type, or system to developing needs, ensures residents' sense of stability.

2) Social Enrichment

Philosophy/Approach: Personal Choice in Activity

The primary consideration concerning social activity is empowering the residents with the freedom and responsibility to partake in the normal activity of choice. This includes being alone, partaking in intimate activity in privacy and with dignity, going out with family, friends, or alone (keeping in mind that special considerations arise with cognitively-impaired residents), or bringing in a family member or friend to visit. This ability to continue to participate in such normal activities and events fosters a consistency of activity and opportunity with the experience and concepts of "home."

Concerning planned activities, a range of normal activities should be considered that allows for social, economic, and service exchanges in smaller and larger groups, both within the facility and outside of the facility. These activities engage the residents with each other, staff, and the community in a manner that allows for a variety of levels of participation (Miller, 1991). Such a range of opportunities provides choices for connecting and belonging that often are difficult for the frail elderly when they are living independently.

Activities that heighten awareness and orientation, and challenge functional abilities without inducing anxiety or need for judgment, respond to the special needs of assisted living residents and provide opportunities for maintenance and expansion of abilities.

3) Psychological Well-Being

Philosophy/Approach (a):
Embrace Homelike Activity and Environment

By affording behaviors and environments that embrace the concepts of home, the primary positive contribution to the psychological well-being of the resident is undertaken. Accommodating and providing opportunities for normal, homelike social engagement that is both enjoyable and purposeful is psychologically therapeutic in itself (Fewster, 1989).

Philosophy/Approach (b):
Address Emotional Issues in Therapy

Many residents enter assisted living residences shortly after suffering the loss of a spouse. The move from a long-time home and into a less-independent setting represents a significant loss as well. It is critical to resident well-being that an active component of the service system be in place to assist residents with the psychological and emotional issues of grief and loss.

Considering cognitively impaired residents, specialized activity may need to be considered that connects the resident to healthy, meaningful, purposeful, and familiar behaviors. These need to be provided in a manner that maintains resident dignity and does not promote segregation. Redundant behavioral and sensory cueing should be employed to layer consistent messages of appropriate activity (Lawton, 1984).

Behavioral Strategies for Integration

Considering the behavioral dimensions of home (activities of daily living, social enrichment, and the psyche) as inherently interactive, the following strategies are derived from the philosophies/approaches that integrate the concepts and services of assisted living with the concepts of home (adapted from Regnier, 1994; Cohen and Weisman, 1991).

1) Consider the Facility the Residents' Household

This forms the foundation of a caregiver–resident relationship relatively equitable to a guest-resident relationship in terms of authority and respect. Attitudes and actions of the staff should reinforce the understanding of the place as the residents' home.

2) Ensure Safety and Security

Along with the responsibility to be alert and responsive, this also implies a careful and thoughtful balance between intervention and informed acceptable risk. A commitment to open communication between staff members, among residents and staff, and with family members should be maintained. Regular interaction with each resident can potentially identify conditions or situations requiring discussion of any change in needs, response, or level of risk.

3) Protect and Respect the Need for Privacy

This applies to the respect of residents' private space (apartment) and private activity. Confidentiality regarding each resident's disabilities, needs, or difficulties is also key to this issue.

4) Maximize Autonomy and Control

This strategy relates most strongly to the caregiver-resident relationship, and empowers the resident as the primary decision-maker. The resident receives assistance as desired, according to their needs and schedules or routines.

5) Inspire Independence and Individuality

Activity that fosters residents' sense of being capable and unique persons should be embraced.

6) Adapt to Changing Needs

Consider each individual resident's set of needs as dynamic, not a static given or necessarily declining condition. Staff should be alert to changes in behavior or ability, and open to discussing potential responses with residents.

7) Heighten Awareness and Orientation

Provide, support, and embrace activity and behavior that reinforces resident orientation to the physical and behavioral organization of the building, the time of day and year, and the happenings and events of the community at large.

8) Support Functional Ability Through Meaningful Activity

Provide opportunities for residents to engage in purposeful activities that embrace, maintain, and challenge their abilities to perform useful tasks and make meaningful decisions that influence significant outcomes. Support their unique and creative talents. Consider their ability to contribute in occupational, social, education, or therapeutic roles that support their sense of purpose and identity. The focus should be on what is and has been productive, enjoyable, and meaningful to them.

9) Establish Links to the Healthy and Familiar

Establish and reinforce resident connection to, and association with, their own physical and emotional well-being. Support their ability to continue to actively engage in activity that reinforces this.

10) Maintain Adaptive Stability, Consistency, and Continuity

The ability for residents to rely on the stability and consistency of their physical and behavioral environment as something known, clear, understood and expected is important to foster a sense of consistency and stability. Also, the consistency and reliability of their relationship with staff is very important in an assisted living environment.

11) Provide Assistance as Needed, Not as Scheduled

Care and service delivery according to individuals' needs and desired routine is the cornerstone of assisted living's service component.

12) Promote Residents' Sense of History, Role, and Place in Time and Community

Provide and embrace opportunities for residents to share their memories, life experience, and important events with each other and the community.

13) Involve Family in Residents' Lives

Afford family members the rights and responsibilities of taking an active role in residents' care and well-being. This includes participation in important decision-making, as well as social and caregiving activity.

14) Layer Consistent Appropriate Behavior Cues

It is important that the ambiance of the environment, the activity taking place in it, and the actions and attitudes of the staff, are consistent in order to reinforce and reiterate cues to appropriate relationships and activity.

15) Provide Meaningful Social, Educational, and Service Exchanges

Provide and support opportunities for residents to be informed of, and engage in, happenings in the world beyond their Assisted Living environment. Activities that engage residents with each other and the community in ways that encourage their contributions should be considered.

16) Provide, Accommodate, and Support a Range of Activity and the Residents' Ability to Choose Levels of Participation

The ability of residents to watch, passively participate, actively participate, or not participate should be fostered.

17) Support and Nurture the Caregiving Staff as an Important and Pivotal Extended Family of the Resident

The importance and value of the work the caregiving staff accomplishes, as well as the relationships they develop with residents, should be acknowledged and supported.

Responsive strategies such as these suggest the potential for not only mitigating the contradictions which are inherent in the integration of the concepts of home with the concepts and services of assisted living residences, but in fact for translating some of these potential contradictions into compliments.

PART III
CONCLUSIONS

CHAPTER 6

ILLUSTRATIVE SOLUTIONS AND CONCLUSIONS

INTRODUCTION

The following two Assisted Living projects, one built and one theoretical, exemplify design responses to the issues and ideas discussed in the Architectural Design Considerations of Chapter Four. They are included to act as vehicles of discussion and inspiration. These two projects illustrate cumulative and comprehensive design solutions which speak of the notions and character of home as integrated with specific site and program requirements and opportunities. They also speak of proactive responses to the special needs of assisted living residents that do not compromise the integrity or quality of home. Architectural solutions are created which synthesize responses to questions of balancing physical needs with the emotional and psychological needs of embracing the concepts and characteristics of home.

The projects herein were selected for their ability to act as complete and comprehensive examples of assisted living architectural design strongly based on a thoughtful and meaningful creation of the homelike environment. Each project is discussed in terms of each design consideration of Chapter Four. A conscious effort was made to select two projects of considerably different (yet reasonable and feasible) scale and context, resulting in a variety of different responses in terms of program, siting, architectural organization and form, and material and detail character.

These solutions are not intended as prototypes, replicable in their entirety in other situations or contexts. The given program and site of each project suggests the most appropriate solutions, and hence renders each individual project unique.

PROJECT ONE: ROSEWOOD ESTATES

Site: Maplewood, Minnesota
Number of Apartments: 79 single-occupancy one-bedroom, 4 two-bedroom, 10 efficiency studios
Square Feet: 88,535
Number of Stories: 3
Architect: BRW Ellness Architects, Inc.

Project Overview

Rosewood Estates is an assisted living facility for 100 residents. Maplewood, the site for Rosewood, is a suburban/rural community in north central Minnesota, outside of Minneapolis/St. Paul.

The harsh Minnesota climate, combined in context with a distributed population, focuses activity and events within the building and naturally de-emphasizes extensive site development or pedestrian accommodation.

The classic architectural building typology of an H-shaped plan establishes a clear organizational and formal system. This formal order creates courtyards between its central axis and wings, and allows the mass of a larger building to be logically articulated into smaller pieces, more closely associated with the mass of a house. (See Figures 6.1., 6.2.)

The amenities offered at Rosewood include a dining room, beauty/barber parlor, a community room, a number of parlor rooms, fireside room with fireplace, greenhouse, home health care office, and four-season porch.

1. Personalizable Entry

Each apartment entry at Rosewood includes a built-in shelf adjacent to the entry door, affording placement of flowers, plants, or other memorabilia.

2. Deconstructed Corridors

Efforts were made, both in plan and section, to erode the long and narrow nature of typical double-loaded corridors. In plan, each corridor edges and opens into a number of shared spaces, including the smaller shared living rooms that occur at the end of each corridor. (See Figure 6.3.) At points along the path, the corridor becomes single-loaded, looking out into small courtyards. In section, a number of overlooks from the corridor occur, from one level down into another. These add unexpected spatial variety in the vertical axis, and provide natural light and interesting previews as one moves along the corridor.

Ground Floor Plan

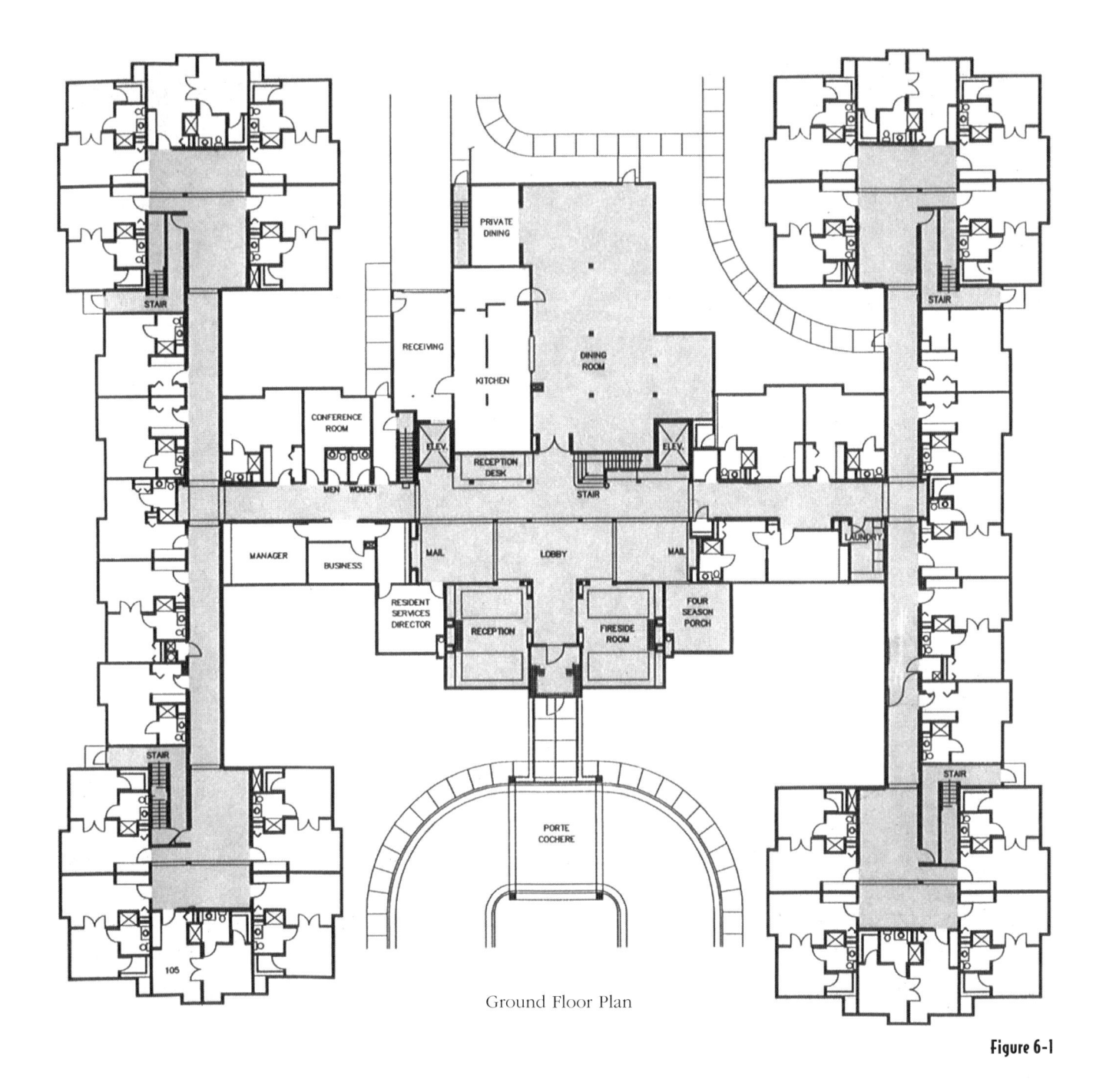

Figure 6-1

3. Refined Material Quality and Spatial Character

The interior colonnade which runs alongside, (and defines) the main corridor space is one element which speaks to a high level of refinement in this project. (See Figure 6.4.) The colonnade clearly delineates the corridor from the shared rooms which often occur adjacent to the corridor, while allowing visual connection and easy access to and from corridor and shared spaces. The columns themselves, finished with base and trim moldings, are refined pieces which relate to a human scale.

Figure 6-2

Figure 6-3

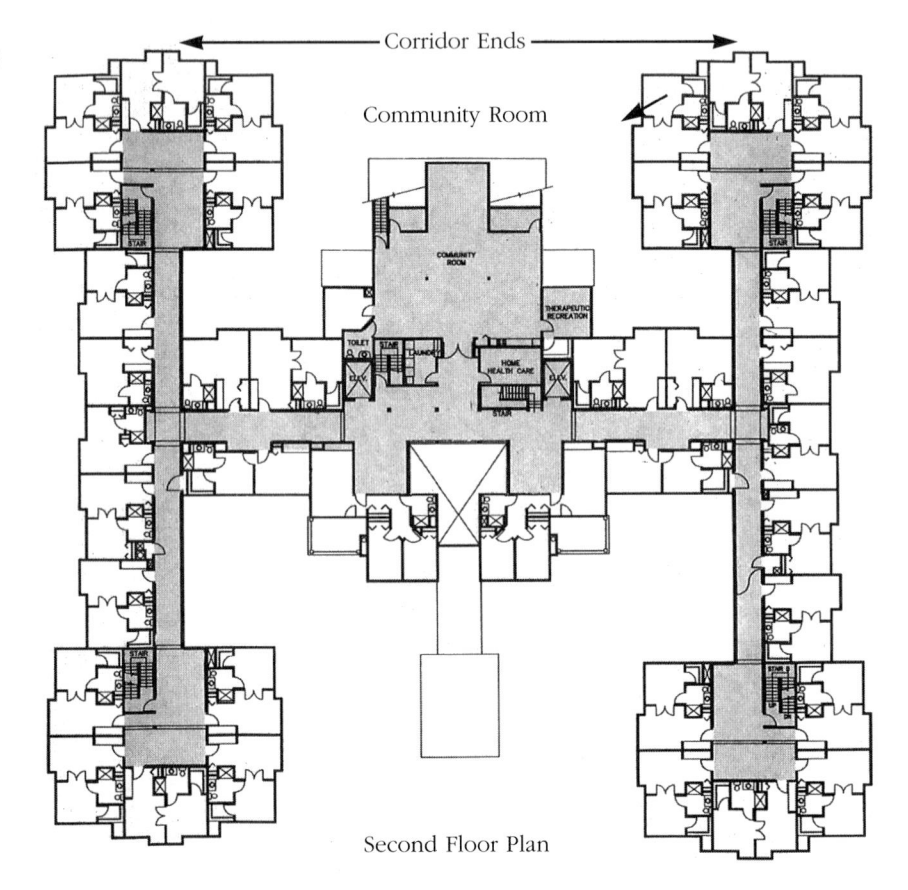

Corridor Ends

Community Room

Second Floor Plan

4. Refined Scale

The articulation of this bay at the four-season porch represents a careful articulation of the building. (See Figure 6.5.) The dormer creates a small piece within a larger roof. Finely detailed railings at the outdoor deck suggest human interaction. French doors and windows have panes which are broken into smaller pieces, again relating to a human scale, creating smaller patterns and rhythms within larger ones

Figure 6-4

5. Community-Integrated Sites

As mentioned in the overview, the context of this facility, one of a harsh climate and nonpedestrian-oriented, de-emphasizes a strong physical relationship of this building to any system of buildings and public circulation within the neighborhood. However, this building does attempt to become an active and working member of the community through its offering of a interior public meeting space, the community room. (See Figure 6.3.)

6. Stages for Community Interaction

The Community Room is offered, free of charge, as a group gathering place for community meetings, gatherings, practices, or events. Such events not only offer opportunities for the residents and community at large to engage one another, but present interesting activities for residents to participate in, or simply watch.

7. Mail Box Event

Mail is received directly adjacent to the main entrance, the Fireside Room, dining room, and main crossing of entry, main corridor, and main stairs. (See Figure 6.1.) Ample space is provided for casual seating in the mail areas, where one may wait for mail and converse with others, or comfortably watch the activity taking place at this grouping of shared spaces.

8. Disguised, Minimized, and Decentralized Parking

Parking at Rosewood is divided into a number of smaller lots. Extensive landscaping diminishes the impact of lots as seen from the street. (See Figure 6.2.)

Figure 6-5

ILLUSTRATIVE SOLUTIONS AND CONCLUSIONS   113

9. Articulated Mass and Form

The H-shaped plan, along with the clustering of apartments at the end of the corridors, very successfully transforms a larger building mass into a series of house forms with proportions and dimensions which are believable as "house." Bays in the facades, such as at the center of the clustered apartments, further articulate the center from edges, main spaces from secondary spaces, and transparent pieces from opaque. (See Figure 6.6.)

10. Private Apartments

Excluding those designed considering residents who wish to share an apartment (4 two-bedroom units), all resident apartments are single-occupancy.

11. Clear Thresholds

The shared living room, which occurs at the end of corridors where apartments are clustered, creates a strong arrival landmark that marks the transition from corridor to apartment. (See Figure 6.1.)

12. Separate Living and Sleeping Areas

All apartments at Rosewood include separate sitting and sleeping areas. In the larger apartments, a separate bedroom is included which can be closed off from the living area by a set of French doors. Smaller efficiency apartments include an alcove large enough to accommodate a bedroom area, somewhat shielded by location from view from the apartment entry. (See Figure 6.7.)

13. Backyard Realm

In addition to reducing the scale of the building, the H-shaped plan creates a series of courtyards between its wings. The courtyards to the back of the building offer opportunities for sitting or strolling during the more pleasant times of the year.

Figure 6-6

Figure 6-7

14. Modified Delivery Place and System

Delivery vehicles enter the building through a residential garage-like receiving area that is sheltered from view and adjacent to the staff kitchen. A vestibule separates the potentially busy area from the resident-occupied spaces. These efforts buffer the receiving area from the facility at large, and clothe an activity of potentially institutional connotations in a residential building atmosphere.

15. Clear and Redundant Order

The plan's symmetry, the clear overall order of the H-shape, and the corridor colonnade together set an order which is very clear, tangible, and comprehensible. Views from the corridor out into courtyards where the corridor becomes single-loaded provide additional visual cues as to the organization of the building and where one is in relationship to it.

Figure 6-8

16. Orienting Entry

The entry to Rosewood occurs at the center of the building. The main corridor, main stairs, and elevator, as well as most major spaces are accessible and visible from the entry. (See Figure 6.8.) Overlooks from the corridor above, which happen near entry, provide additional clarity regarding what rooms and events occur at the second level.

17. Continuous and Connecting Circulation Route

The design of the circulation system, which arrives at ample shared spaces, creates a natural place for walkers or those who may wander, to stop and rest or converse, or loop around the space and continue.

18. Layered Building Envelope

The facade of each group of apartments is layered from the center of the cross gable. At the outermost layer, a narrow balcony edge extends in front of French doors. A small bay at the first and second levels is at the center of the cross gable, while behind the bay the cross gable itself articulates the center of the building piece. (See Figure 6.2.)

19. Private Outdoor Space

The frequently inclement weather of this region somewhat diminishes the value of outdoor spaces, particularly for the frail. This issue, therefore, being a low priority in the given context, was not addressed.

20. Useful Kitchenette

All resident apartments include fully equipped kitchenettes.

ILLUSTRATIVE SOLUTIONS AND CONCLUSIONS

21. Personally Adjustable Apartment Controls

All resident apartments have individual heating, ventilation, and lighting controls. Apartment doors lock and are equipped with a master keyhole accessible to the staff in case of emergency.

22. Easy Adaptability to Changing Needs

The French doors between the bedroom and living room in resident apartments are an architectural feature which is very easily adaptable. Doors can be closed and curtains on French door glazing can be pulled shut to provide optimal privacy. For residents who may not need or desire such separation, the French doors can be opened fully, providing maximum visual and physical access. (See Figure 6.7.)

23. Ample and Unencumbered Spaces with Support

The wide corridors at Rosewood are lined with a chair rail along each side. This rail is designed with a top surface that acts as a support for those who may feel unsteady while walking the corridor. (See Figure 6.9.) Although this element provides a relatively continuous place of support, its appearance is one of a normal chair rail which may occur in a home.

24. Responsive Elements and Hardware

Along with the typically specified lever doorknobs, special consideration was given to door-closing hardware at Rosewood. Although fire safety regulations stipulated that doors from resident rooms into the corridor must have automatic closers, standard closers required too much force for many residents to comfortably operate. An adjustable closer was used in lieu of the standard type, allowing staff or resident to easily adjust the required force needed to operate the door, to the abilities of each individual apartment owner.

Figure 6-9

25. Push, Pull, Test, and Reinterpret Restrictions and Regulations

The same issue of fire safety required thresholds at all doors from resident rooms into corridors. Unfortunately, thresholds can often be obstacles to those in wheelchairs or using walkers. At Rosewood, the decision was made to eliminate thresholds, providing certain fire-resistive qualities were met by the carpeting used in the corridor. This ensured that the problem of fire entering apartments from corridors, which thresholds helped prevent, was addressed by other means which did not limit resident access.

26. Unobtrusive Reception-Observation

The receptionist at Rosewood sits behind a unassuming desk, adjacent to the lobby, main stairs, main corridor, and dining room. The role of the receptionist, as well as the ambiance of the reception area, is one of a greeter, as opposed to an administrator or caregiver. The reception place and activity thus becomes associated with social courtesies rather than control.

27. Normalized and Positive Bathing

A side-entry tub is used in Rosewood, which approximates a much more normal character and process for entering the tub than many other assisted bathing apparatuses.

28. Purposeful Exterior Rooms

Two distinct site elements were created which provide different outdoor settings and suggest different types of engagement. A small flower garden with a wandering path provides opportunities for residents to tend flowers in the warmer summer months. (See Figure 6.10.) Further away from the building, in a more quiet and private

Figure 6-10

outdoor setting, a gazebo provides a comfortable space for sitting and reading or talking while protected from the sun.

29. Central Dining with Intimate Scale

Alcoves and spaces within the larger dining space are created by introducing columns, soffits, and low walls in the dining room. Its location, directly adjacent to the main open stairs and main corridor, fosters the aspects of dining as a rich social event, tied to the heart of the facility, rather than a barren cafeteria-type room separated from the rest of the facility.

30. Casual Preview

The many overlooks from the main corridor at the second level down into the first, such as occur at the two-story lobby space, offer opportunities for preview of activities and enable residents to more comfortably choose participation or nonparticipation. (See Figure 6.8.)

31. Eventful and Enjoyable Stairway

The main stairs open to the entry space, mail room, and main lobby, and are visually connected through interior windows or open columnation to the fireside room, four season porch, dining room, and reception area. The stairs themselves are positioned prominently at the center of the building, inviting use. (See Figures 6.1, 6.8.)

32. Places for Enjoyable Rest

The ample corridors, and shared spaces which frequently open off of them, provide opportunities for furniture placement. These smaller-and medium-sized spaces become locations for comfortable rest and conversation as one walks along the corridor.

33. Living Room Activity Spaces

Two larger rooms, in addition to the dining room and community room, were developed with homelike themes and architectural elements. The reception parlor and fireside room offer larger, yet residentially scaled settings for residents to gather or receive and entertain guests. A fireplace, built-in book cases, and generous windows establish a warm and homelike ambiance in the first rooms experienced when entering the building. (See Figure 6.4.)

34. Small and Comfortable Shared Spaces

The shared living rooms created at each cluster of apartments offers a setting for neighbors to visit. A number of other smaller themed rooms, such as the greenhouse, four-season porch, and beauty parlor, suggest enriching activity closely associated with home and community. (See Figure 6.11.)

35. Engaging Activity Kitchen

Within the community room, a fully equipped kitchen space serves as a gathering spot for residents and staff to participate in simple cooking and baking. This also acts as a serving kitchen for events held in the community room.

36. Laundry as a Multisensory Experience

The laundry room is included as one of the activity and shared spaces at the center of the facility. Residents' accessibility to this location is relatively easy, and fosters the connection of their home with a place where such normal activities, such as as doing laundry, occur. (See Figure 6.11). An interior window between corridor and laundry room visually connect the two, even when the door is closed to control sound.

37. Adaptive Office Connection

The size of this facility, serving 100 residents, requires a service component that is relatively complex. Rather than having a few staff members who complete a wide variety of tasks, as is often the case in smaller facilities, the tasks are specialized. This specialization allows one person, such as the receptionist, to focus exclusively on interactions with residents and overseeing the general security of the building, while others focus on administrative or caregiving activities. This arrangement dimishes the importance of this design consideration.

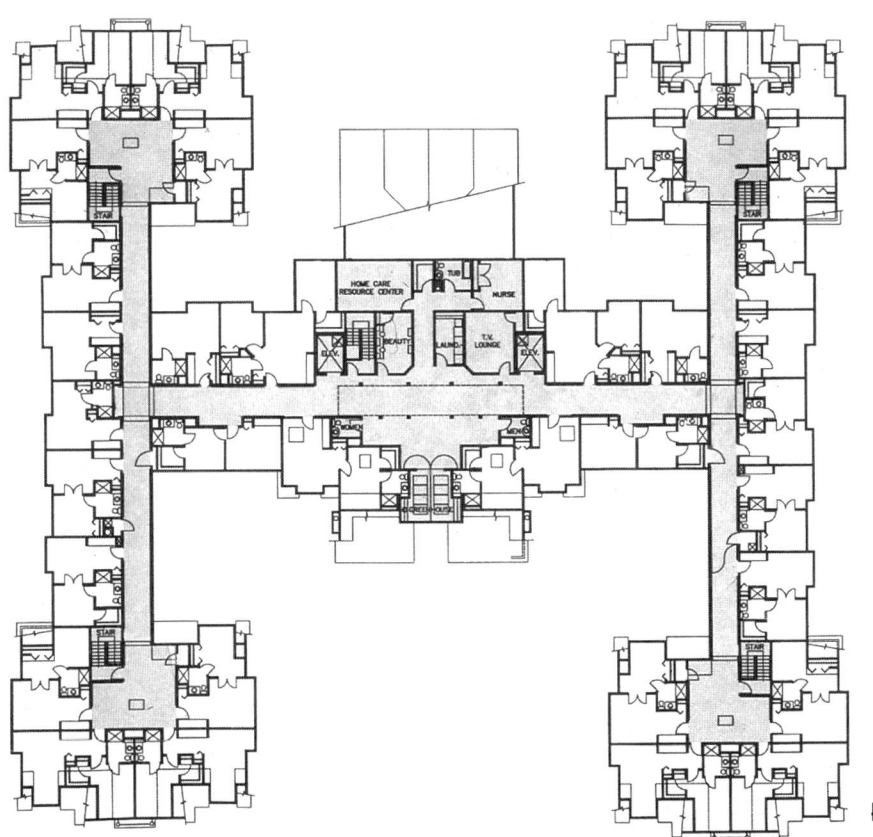

Figure 6-11

Project Two: CORVALLIS ASSISTED LIVING

Site: Corvallis, Oregon
Number of Apartments: 30 single-occupancy, 3 double-occupancy, two-bedroom
Square Feet: 37,821
Number of Stories: 3
Architect: William Brummett

Project Overview

This theoretical project is located in Corvallis, Oregon (population 50,000), which is roughly 50 miles south of Portland, nestled between the foothills of the Coast Range and the west bank of the Willamette River. The four-to-six-story historical brick-and-stone downtown (approximately six blocks by twelve blocks) rests at the edge of the river. Eight blocks directly west of downtown, and connected to the town's center by Madison Street, is Oregon State University (approximately 12,000 students).

Corvallis Assisted Living's site is along the south edge of Madison Street, two blocks west of downtown, and diagonally adjacent to the main city park. (See Figure 6.12.)

The building itself is organized to form a south-facing courtyard. A larger building wing to the east, facing the city, houses the larger program pieces (such as the dining room) while bays of two resident apartments are articulated along the north and west facades. A strong corner piece, which houses a public and resident-shared coffee house, addresses the park. (See Figures 6.13, 6.14, 6.15.)

Shared spaces at Corvallis Assisted Living include a dining/living room, den, library, breakfast room on the park, activity kitchen, assisted bathing room, and staff office and retreat.

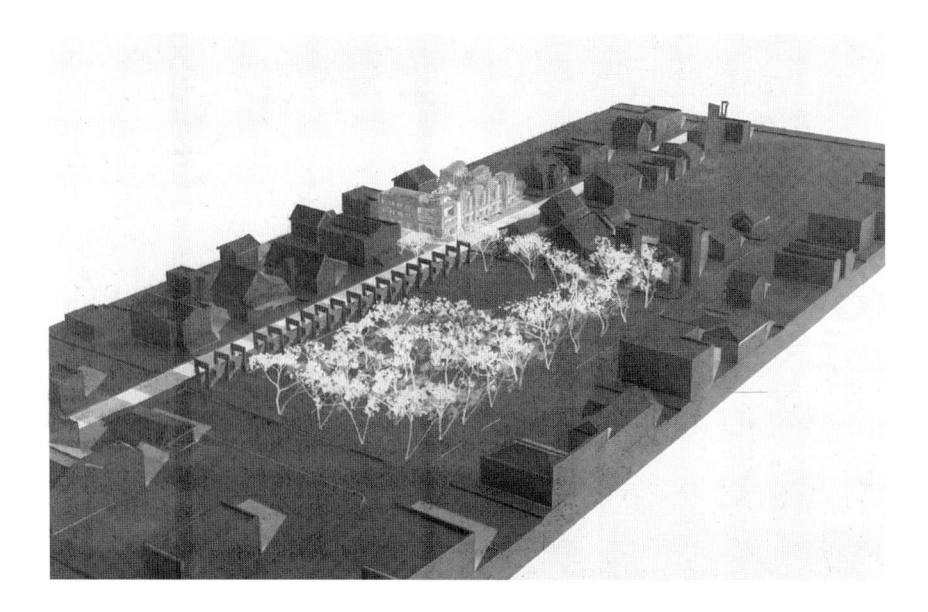

Figure 6-12 *Areal view across park to Corvallis Assisted Living.*

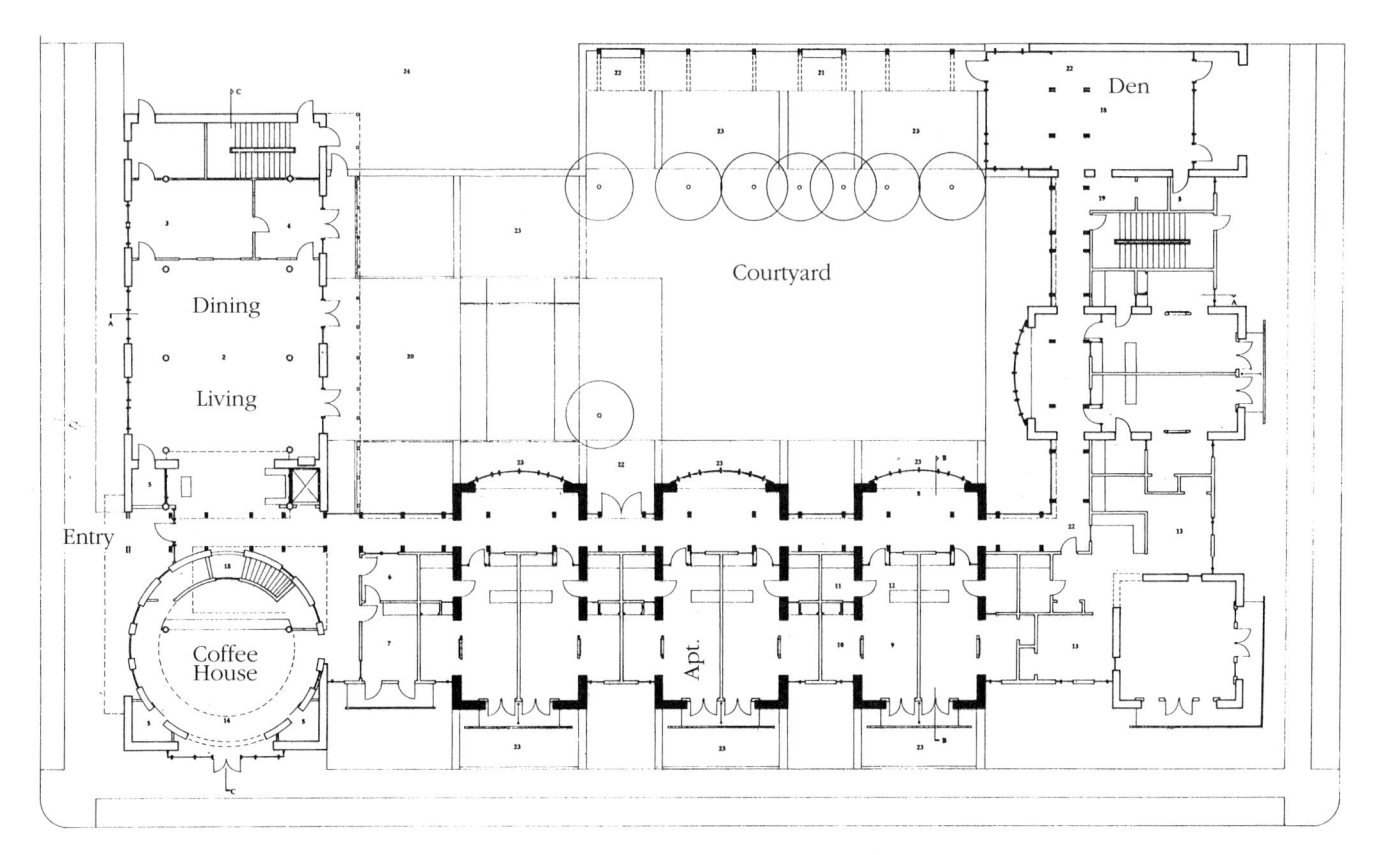

Figure 6-13

1. Personalizable Entry

Apartment entries occur in setbacks from the corridor which act as entry porches looking out to the south-facing courtyard beyond. (See Figure 6.16.) This affords the placement of perhaps a small table and chair or two, potted plants, or other personal items. Additionally, interior windows with deep sills between corridor and kitchen, at apartment entries, afford display of memorabilia.

2. Deconstructed Corridors

The single-loaded corridor is flooded with natural light, due to extensive glazing looking into the courtyard. The brick walls of apartment bays carry through the corridor, creating a pleasing rhythm of masonry spaces along the circulation route. (See Figure 6.13). These two conditions transform a typical linear and enclosed corridor into what is essentially an "outdoor" room, full of natural light and views, and sequenced by clear and powerful brick bays.

3. Refined Material and Spatial Quality

The wood-clad drum at the site's corner is one element of this project which speaks of this issue. Materially, the drum's cladding, Myrtle wood, is a semi-precious resource found almost exclusively in Corvallis' Willamette Valley, and is hence historically and culturally connected with the value and meaning of the town. Spatially, its form, a cylinder, is a unique landmark, noting entry, main stairs, main circulation crossing, and the building's important connection to the park (diagonally from corner). (See Figure 6.17.)

4. Refined Scale

The articulation of apartment bays (two apartments grouped back to back), both in form and through a change in material from cedar siding to brick, visually reduce the perceived scale of this building, which might otherwise appear relatively large in its context. (See Figure 6.14.) These bays were designed in cross section to address the different scales of the courtyard on one side, and the street on the other. A shorter facade faces the courtyard and stronger southern sun. Curving up in section to a taller street facade, the opposite side of the building accepts generous amounts of soft northern light. (See Figure 6.18.)

5. Community-Integrated Sites

Appropriate site selection was a paramount concern for this project. Careful study yielded the chosen site near the heart of the community. Corvallis Assisted Living is located along the main pedestrian avenue, directly adjacent to the main city park, and within a short walking distance to the shops and restaurants of the city, the public library, the town's civic center, four churches, and a major university. (See Figure 6.19.)

6. Stages for Community Interaction

The program for Corvallis Assisted Living was created to include a casual coffee house, inviting and open to the community at large. This is situated on the corner of the site, adjacent to the park, and along the main pedestrian street. The coffee house is accessed direct-

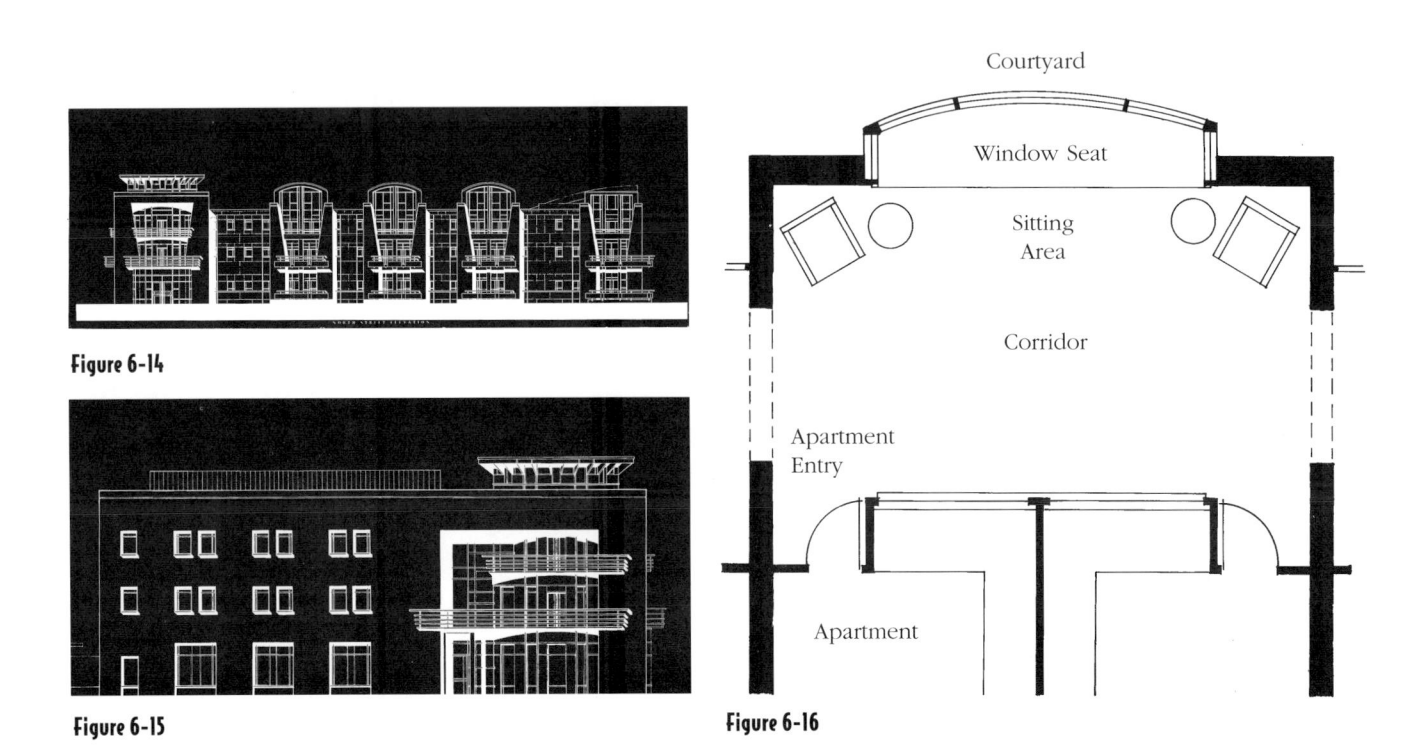

Figure 6-14

Figure 6-15

Figure 6-16

Figure 6-17

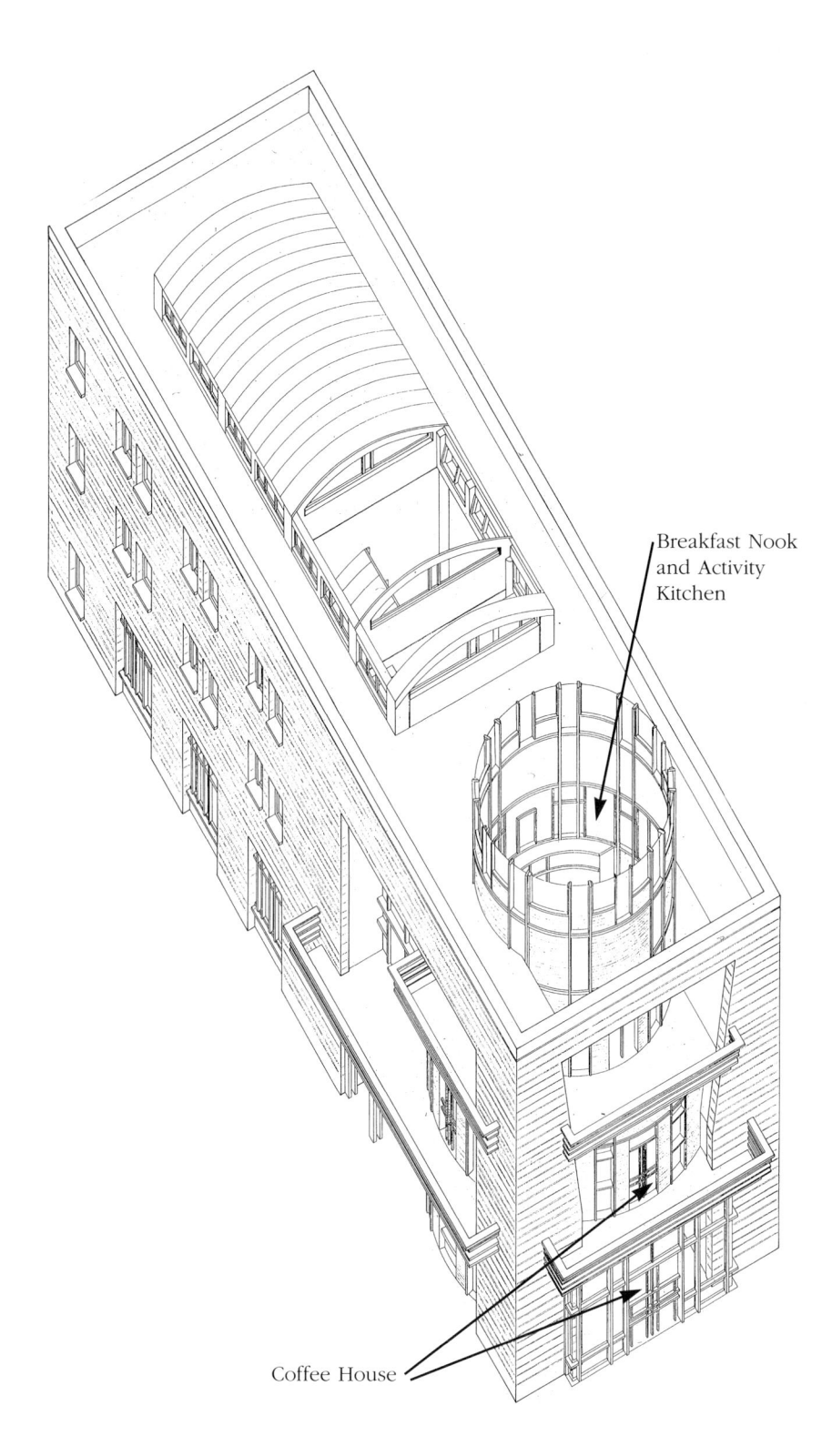

ly from the street, and from within the facility. The main stairs move up along an edge of the coffee house, affording casual overlooks into the activity of this shared setting, as well as comfortable layered access. (See Figure 6.20.)

ILLUSTRATIVE SOLUTIONS AND CONCLUSIONS

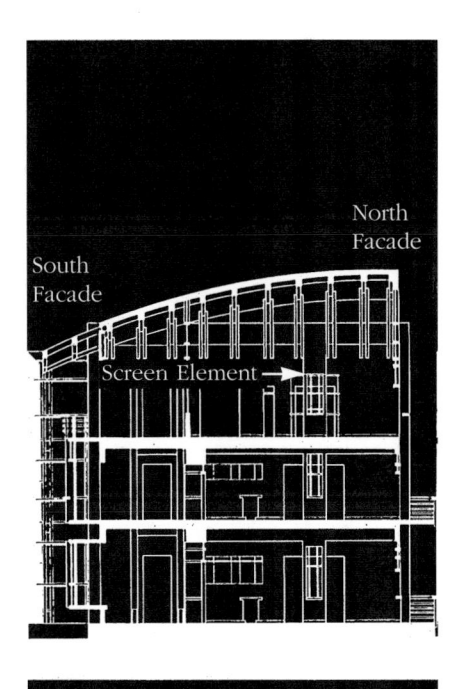

Figure 6-18

7. Mailbox Event

Resident mailboxes are located directly adjacent to the entry, main stairs and corridor, and dining area. Space for sitting and conversing is afforded near the mailbox, to accommodate resident interaction around this positive, engaging, and orienting daily event. (See Figure 6.21).

8. Disguised, Minimized, and Decentralized Parking

Parking at Corvallis Assisted Living is kept to a minimum. The local residential pattern is continued, with only a few distinct on-site parking spaces created for staff and deliveries. The remainder of parking is curbside, as is typical in this residential context. The few on-site spaces are kept behind the building, off of the alley adjacent to the service entry. This minimizes the impact of an unsightly and contextually inconsistent parking lot, while maximizing the amount of space available to create an ample shared courtyard. (See Figure 6.13.) A variance in town planning regulations would enable such a deviation from the typically mandated number of parking spaces.

9. Articulated Mass and Form

An overall design strategy which intended to reflect the different scales of the immediate context was developed. To the sites' east, the somewhat larger buildings of the town proper suggested creating a

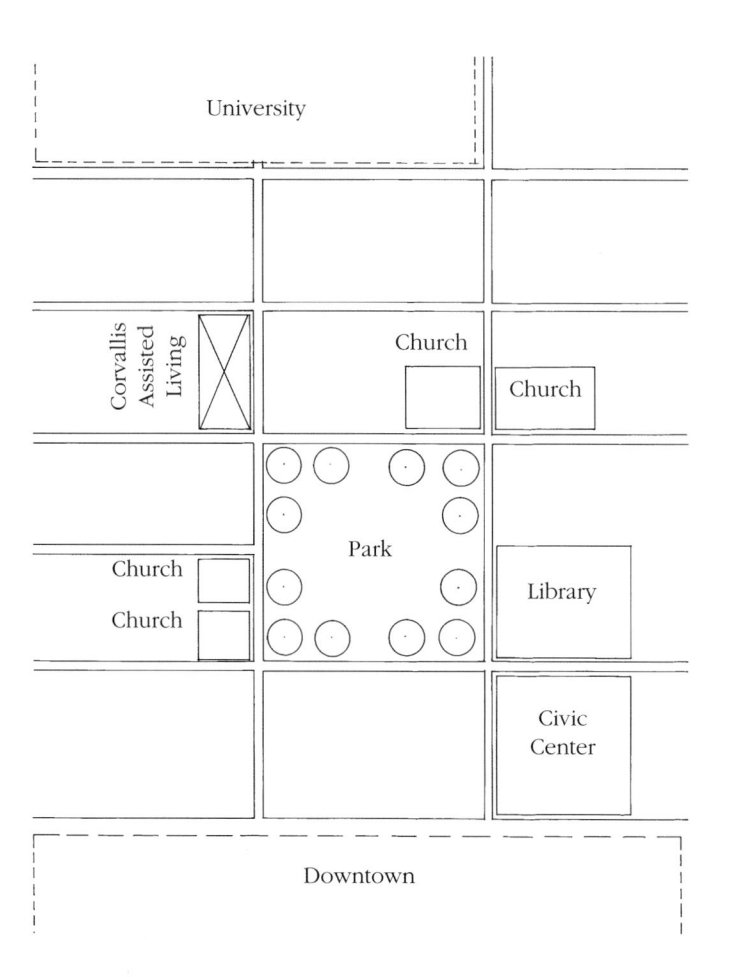

Figure 6-19

124   THE ESSENCE OF HOME

larger building piece to match the scale of these larger buildings and to house some of the larger rooms of the facility, such as the dining room. The articulation of the apartment bays along the north and west site edges respects the smaller, two to three-story residential scale along these adjacencies. The special corner piece, the wood-clad drum housing the coffee house creates a formal transition piece between the larger building and the articulated apartment bays. (See Figure 6.14.)

10. Private Apartments

With the exception of three apartments intended for two residents to share, all resident apartments are single-occupancy.

11. Clear Thresholds

The thick and heavy masonry walls of the apartment bays create clear and powerful thresholds in a number of different places and architectural situations throughout the building. As residents move through the corridor, crossing masonry walls create a rhythm which announces apartment porch alcoves and entries. Within each apartment, the same thick brick walls separate the public and private areas of the apartment. Bedroom and bath are on one side of the masonry "threshold," while entry, kitchenette, and living room are on the other side. (See Figure 6.16.)

12. Separate Living and Sleeping Areas

Each resident apartment includes either an ample bedroom alcove or a separate bedroom. The sleeping alcove is separated from the living area of the apartment by a partial wood "screen wall" with windows. This affords easy access and adaptable visual connection

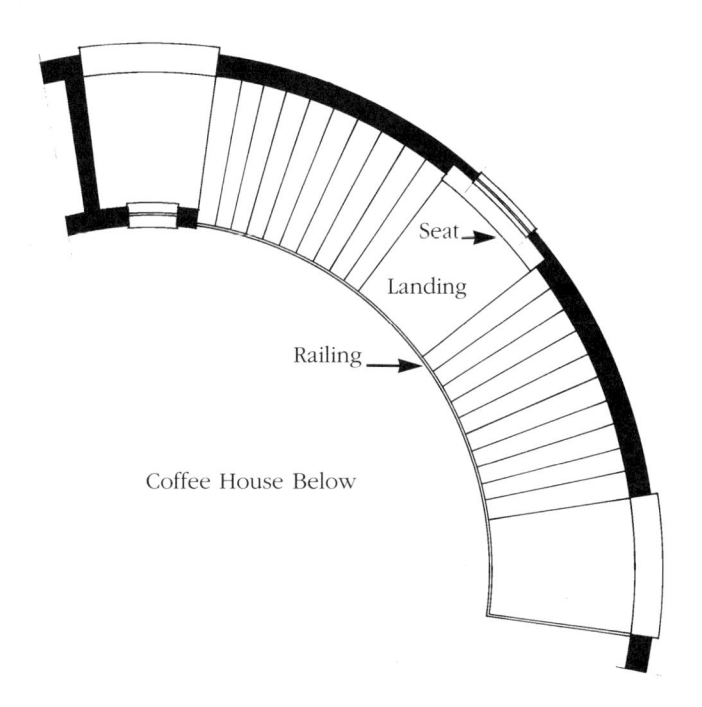

Figure 6-20

Figure 6-21

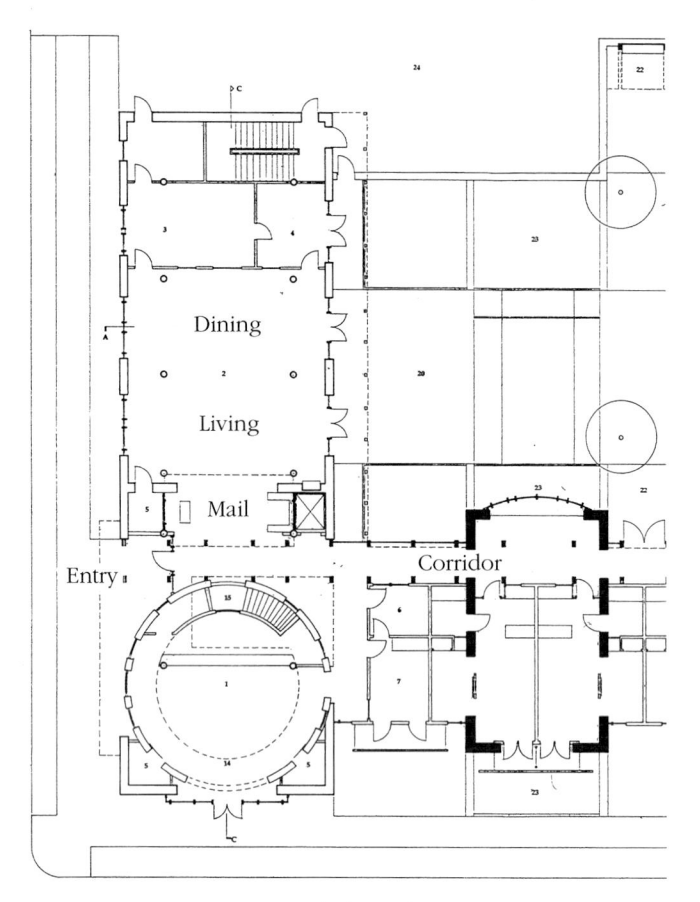

Partial Floor Plan

between the two areas, while maintaining the necessary privacy and distinction between the semipublic and private areas of the apartment. (See Figures 6.16, 6.18.)

13. Backyard Realm

The south-facing, enclosed courtyard provides an outdoor space for residents and visitors to gather and socialize, or engage in gardening, outdoor dining, or walking. The south fence and pergola, a trellised arbor, complete the enclosure of the courtyard, creating a safe and semi-private realm while blocking noise and views to and from the alley. (See Figure 6.13.)

14. Modified Delivery Place and System

Goods and supplies deliveries occur through a back "mud room," adjacent to the service kitchen. This approach of utilizing an unobtrusive delivery entrance maintains the desired lower profile for delivery activity, from both the outside residential neighborhood and from within the building. (See Figure 6.13.)

15. Clear and Redundant Order

The basic architectural part of this project, a single-loaded (corridor) building arranged about a courtyard, establishes a clear and archetypal order. Circulating through the corridor, and from apartment interior windows, orienting views to the courtyard are omnipresent. The corner drum, whether viewed from within or without, acts as a clear and unique landmark. These two elements combine to establish a clear organization and a special and powerful landmark. (See Figure 6.22.)

16. Orienting Entry

Resident entry to the building occurs near the corner drum, at a clear juncture between the drum and the larger piece of the building. Once inside, one is on axis with the main corridor, directly adjacent to, and in clear view of, the shared dining/living area, reception desk, main stairs and elevator, and mailboxes, and with a view through the corridor glazing to the remainder of the building beyond. At the point of entry, all possible paths and destinations are clear. (See Figure 6.13.)

17. Continuous and Connecting Circulation Route

The circumnavigating corridor of the building begins and ends at resident-shared spaces. At the beginning of the corridor (near the entry), the dining and living rooms, mailboxes, and coffee house are all adjacent. At the end of the corridor, a resident-shared den is created. This organization provides orienting activity spaces which mark significant transitions in the path. At the exterior, the path is continued and completed by a walking path and pergola along the south edge, which leads to the dining terrace, dining room and, eventually, back to the corridor. (See Figure 6.13).

18. Layered Building Envelope

The north and west facades of the building incorporate a number of changes in plane, material, and wall transparency in an effort to

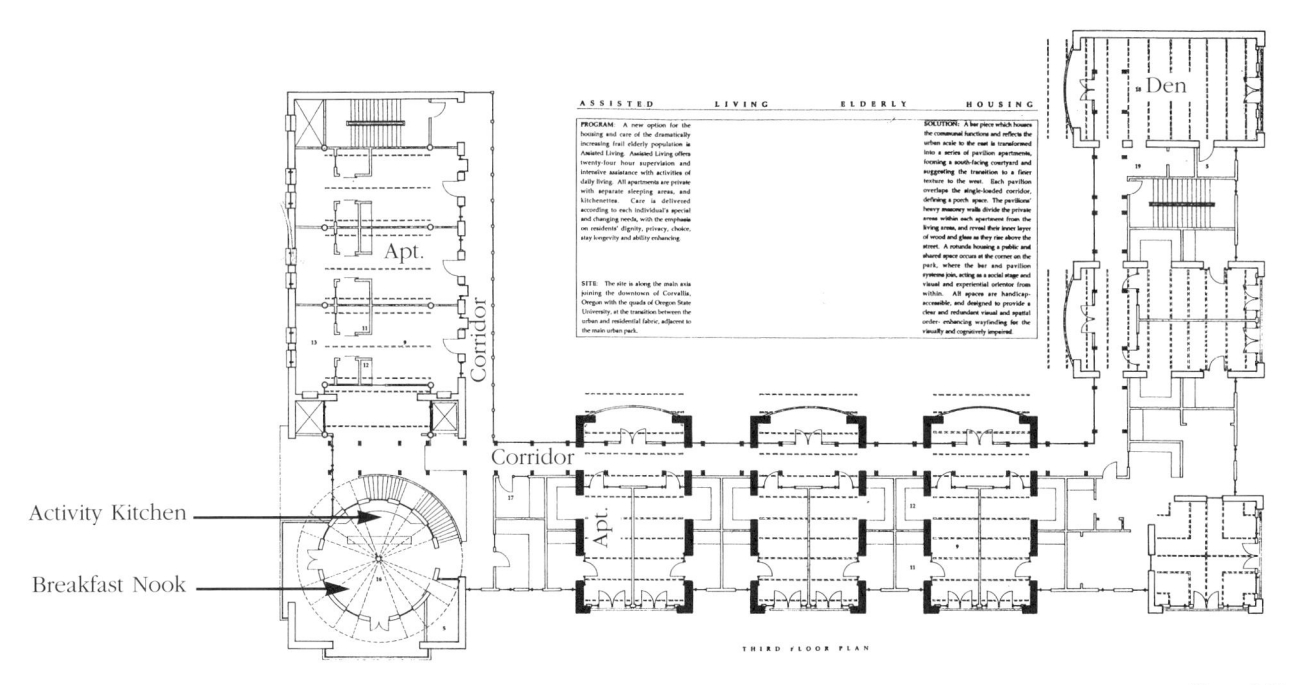

Figure 6-22

buffer the potentially active street from the inner private realm, as well to as create an interesting and residentially scaled facade. The more public apartment living rooms are in front, toward to the street. Their facades are more glazed as one moves higher in the building, as privacy from passersby in the street becomes less of a concern. A small deck from each living room protrudes a bit more toward the street. The most-private areas, the bedrooms, are behind the living rooms, and have smaller and higher sills. (See Figures 6.14, 6.23.)

19. Private Outdoor Space

Apartments at Corvallis Assisted Living include a small yet comfortable terrace off of the living rooms. This accommodates residents who wish to enjoy the outdoors privately (from their units), and affords casual and familiar activity such as sitting on a porch and watching the activity of the street and park.

20. Useful Kitchenette

Every apartment includes a small, fully equipped kitchenette. This includes a refrigerator, electric stove and oven (and/or microwave), sink, cabinets, and counter space. Progressive Oregon laws require equipped kitchenettes in all assisted living apartments—a formal recognition of the import and value of such a feature.

21. Personally Adjustable Apartment Controls

Each apartment has its own separate heating, ventilation, and lighting controls. Apartment doors lock and feature a master keyhole which can be accessed in emergencies by a master key under supervisor control.

22. Easy Adaptability to Changing Needs

Within resident apartments, the kitchenettes are one element which include features which can be easily adapted to changes in abilities or desires. The electric stove is designed and located to allow for relatively simple staff disconnection or removal. It may then be possible to replace the stove with either a microwave oven or simply a work surface.

23. Ample and Unencumbered Spaces with Support

A chair rail designed to act as a handrail-like support unobtrusively lines the main corridor, providing a solid element on which to lean or steady oneself, while still maintaining the appearance of a feature common to many homes.

24. Responsive Elements and Hardware

Cabinets, window seats, shelving, and other work and rest surfaces were designed to be responsive to residents' diminished abilities to stoop low, stretch far, or reach high.

Figure 6-23

25. Push, Pull, Test, and Reinterpret Regulations

Since the state of Oregon has very progressive laws supporting the better models of Assisted Living, very few issues presented themselves as regulatory obstacles. However, local planning regulations required a number of parking spaces inappropriate and excessive for an assisted living population or the context of the neighborhood. In order to limit the number of on-site spaces, a variance would have to be sought.

26. Unobtrusive Reception-Observation

No formal, built-in reception element was created in Corvallis Assisted Living. This was the result of careful and deliberate consideration. In lieu, an area for a furniture piece, such as a desk, was allocated adjacent to, but not in direct path of, the entry, main spaces, and horizontal and vertical circulation. (See Figure 6.21.)

27. Normalized and Positive Bathing

Normal-looking side-entry tubs were selected for the assisted bathing rooms in an effort to minimize the awkwardness of this activity. Interior windows with blinds and curtains between bathing room and entry way from the corridor cue staff and residents of use, as the blinds are closed when the room is occupied.

28. Purposeful Exterior Rooms

A number of themes, relating to normal homelike activity were developed in the design of the courtyard in an effort to cue behavior and engagement. The west-facing dining terrace supports summer barbecues around umbrellaed tables. Raised planting beds allow for gardening, even by those in wheelchairs or unable to comfortably reach the ground. The pergola along the southwest edge of the site provides a comfortable place to sit outdoors, overlooking the garden, while protected from the sun, wind, and rain. (See Figure 6.13.)

29. Central Dining with Intimate Scale

The projects' dining area is located just off of the main horizontal and vertical circulation paths, near the main stairs and entry. Alcoves created by interior columns provide subspaces within the larger dining room, suggesting placement of tables for smaller groups of diners. (See Figure 6.13.)

30. Casual Preview

The arrangement of shared spaces, such as the dining room, coffee house, courtyard, and den, off of the main corridor, allows residents who may be walking by to comfortably continue their stroll or choose to enter a room and participate in the activity within. Extensive use of interior windows, such as between apartment kitchens and corridor, accommodates casual preview as well.

31. Eventful and Enjoyable Stairway

The main stairs of this project wrap around and through the coffee house drum, and land ceremonially on axis with the dining/living room. As one moves up the stairs, views down into the coffee house, as well as into the main corridor and active rooms, are offered. The stairs thus becomes a powerful architectural element, engaging users and providing visual connection to activities and events. (See Figures 6.14, 6.22.)

32. Places for Enjoyable Rest

A built-in seat is offered at the midlanding of the main stair, with views into the coffee house. This presents an enjoyable place to rest and converse along the route. Window seats along the corridor, opposite apartment entries and looking into the courtyard, act as resting spaces off of the path, inviting residents to sit and talk. (See Figure 6.24.)

33. Living Room Activity Spaces

The main space of this project is located at the heart of the facility, adjacent to the main horizontal and vertical circulation routes and near the entry. This room opens west to the courtyard through a series of French doors, becoming the most public and active space fully engaging the courtyard.

34. Small and Comfortable Shared Spaces

A number of themes drove the development of a variety of smaller resident-shared spaces. A breakfast room occupies the corner drum at the third level, above the coffee house, looking onto the park. A quieter den space occurs at the far end of the corridor, away from the very active entry, yet engaged by the corridor. At a small scale, the corridor window seats provide more intimate settings for two or three to socialize.

35. Engaging Activity Kitchen

The resident- and staff-shared activity kitchen occurs in conjunction with the breakfast room on the third level of the corner drum. It acts not only as a therapeutic activity setting (activity kitchen and craft area), but doubles as a small serving kitchen for breakfasts or other small dining events which may want to take full advantage of the park views.

36. Laundry as a Multisensory Experience

The laundry room occurs at the second and third floors, along the main corridor of the facility, near the main stairs and overlook to the entry and mail. This location allows the laundry room to become another contributor to, and receptor of, the activity that is grouped at the circulation crossing. Interior windows between corridor and laundry maintain visual connection while controlling sound.

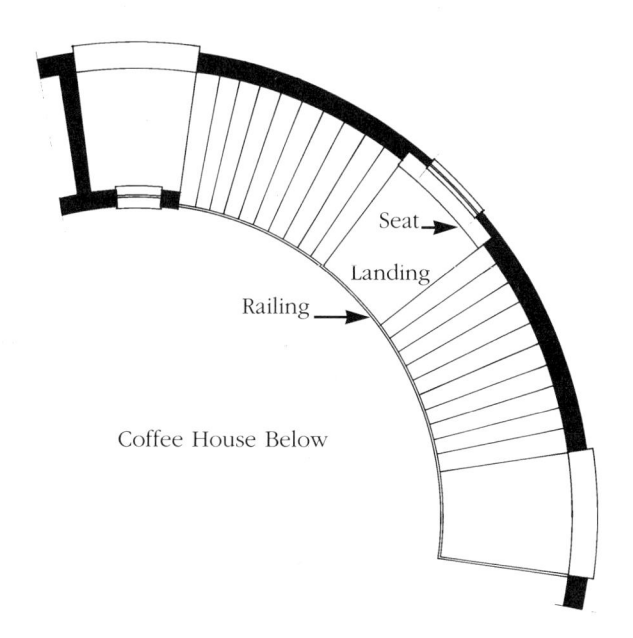

Figure 6-24

37. Adaptive Office Connection

The staff office is located diagonally across from the reception desk, adjacent to the main corridor and main stair crossing. Interior windows from office into the corridor and main space allow a staff member to open windows and engage residents, work quietly with doors closed (while maintaining visual connection to the facility through closed windows), or close curtains and maintain concentrated efforts.

CONCLUSIONS

Solutions to elderly housing design that truly and wholly embrace the character of home hold great potential for improving the quality of the last years of people's lives. More and more people face the painful predicament each day of needing housing and care for a frail loved one, and finding the only options available are environments that foster a sense of *loss* of dignity, self-reliance, and wellness.

As more options for care and housing for the frail, semi-independent elderly that are founded on creating homelike environments develop, the opportunities for continuing a rich, productive, dignified, valuable, and meaningful life expand and eclipse other custodial, institutional alternatives which are now becoming understood as much less than ideal.

The weight of this potential becomes even more poignant when understood in the context of the exponentially increasing numbers of those who are and will be in need of such care and housing. The realization that the extent of this semi-independent phase of life is dramatically increasing, and that the typical length of the fully dependent life phase is decreasing, amplifies the intensity of the need to aggressively pursue the better options of elderly housing.

The medical and social constituent professions involved in elderly well-being have responded to this need. Evolved theories and philosophies in these fields are yielding approaches to the care and enrichment of the lives of our elders which consider the *quality* of life paramount.

It is indeed time to reconsider and evolve the other important aspect of the equation of continuing a healthy, enriching, and meaningful existence: the built environment.

This requires a thoughtful and conscious effort. It is necessary to rethink and reevaluate many of the initially and generally accepted approaches to the design of elderly housing. What was once a given, and has been institutionalized through decades of practice as well as regulation, is now becoming understood as misunderstanding. A hospital or institutional building organization and typological model does not and cannot yield appropriate nor desirable housing. The only appropriate model which must be restudied, adapted, and abstracted is *home* itself.

This rethinking process, which is necessary to avoid these ingrained traditions of creating institutional settings, begins with asking the question, "What are the aspects of home which are integral to the notion 'home' that can remain purposeful, appropriate, and relevant in an assisted living environment?" This work attempts to continue and advance this line of questioning.

In order to render the process and eventual product of this rethinking rich, meaningful, and lasting, it is necessary to reconsider the very conceptual foundations of the notion of home, not merely its resultant image. The concepts and the design issues and considerations which make the concepts manifest, hold the key to reaching relatively unlimited architectural solutions which resonate with the depth and breadth of the essence of *home*.

APPENDIX A

BIBLIOGRAPHY

Assisted Living Specific

American Academy for Hospital Architecture (AAHA). 1992. Assisted Living State Code Workbook, Washington, D.C.

American Association of Retired Persons (AARP). 1993. Assisted Living In The U.S.: A New Paradigm For Residential Care for Frail Older Persons, Washington, D.C.: Public Policy Institute.

Bowe, J. 1993. "Medicaid Takes the Plunge into Assisted Living." *Contemporary Long Term Care.* September. V9, pp. 26–31.

Brummett, William J. 1993. Interviews of 37 residents of assisted living facilities. May through August.

___. 1992. Assisted Living: A Working Definition and Resident Needs Assessment. Milwaukee: University of Wisconsin/Milwaukee. Unpublished paper.

Bowe, J. 1993. "Architectural, Design Awards." *Contemporary Long Term Care.* June. Vol. 16, #6, pp. 41–61.

Bowe, J. 1993. "Bolder Design Solutions Needed." *Contemporary Long Term Care.* June. Vol. 16, #6, pp. 62–64.

Donahue, W. T.; Pepe, H; and Murray, P. 1988. Assisted Independent Living in Residential Congregate Housing: A Report on the Situation in the U.S. International Center for Social Gerontology.

Hendrickson, M. 1988. "Assisted Living: An Emerging Focus in an Expanding Market." *Contemporary Long Term Care.* July, pp. 20, 22.

Hoglund, D. 1985. Housing for the Elderly: Privacy and Independence in Environments for the Aging. New York: Van Nostrand Reinhold.

Kane, R., Illuston L., and Nyman, J. 1990. Meshing Services with Housing: Lessons From Adult Foster Care and Assisted Living in Oregon.

___. 1987. "Quality of Life in Long-Term Institutions: Is a Regulatory Strategy Feasible?" *Danish Medical Bulletin*. Oct., Supplement 5: 73–81.

Kalymum, M. 1992. "Board and Care Versus Assisted Living: Ascertaining the Similarities and Differences." *Adult Residential Care Journal*. Vol. 6 (1), pp. 35–44.

___. 1990. Toward a Definition of Assisted Living. *In Optimizing Housing for the Elderly: Homes Not Housing,* ed. L. Pastalan, 97–132. New York: The Hayworth Press, Inc.

Long Term Care National Resource Center at UCLA/USC. 1989. *Assisted Living Resource Guide*. Los Angeles.

Miller, J. A., and Patten, T. M. 1991. "Generations Assisted Living Homes: Miller-Dawn Medical Center, Duluth, Minnesota." *In Community-Based Long Term Care: Innovative Models,* ed. J. A. Miller, 174–188. Newbury Park, CA: Sage Publications.

___. 1991. "Concepts in Community Living Assisted Living Program, Portland, Oregon." *In Community-Based Long Term Care. Innovative Models,* ed. J. A. Miller, 174–188. Newbury Park, CA: Sage Publications.

Mullen, A. J. 1991. "The Assisted-Living Industry: An Assessment." *Retirement Housing Report*. January. V1, pp. 42–47.

Pristic, S. 1991. "Assisted Living in the Spotlight: New Association Eyes Expanding Medicaid Funding." *Contemporary Long Term Care*. Feb., pp. 40–42.

Regnier, V. 1994. *Assisted Living Housing for the Elderly: Design Innovations from the United States and Europe*. New York: Van Nostrand Reinhold.

___. 1992. *European Models of Assisted Living Housing for Mentally and Physically Frail Older People*. Running Time—95 minutes, width 3/4. Los Angeles: Andrus Gerontology Center, USC.

___. 1992. "Focus on Assisted Living." *Supporting Housing Options*. Summer. Los Angeles: National Eldercare Institute on Housing and Supportive Services, pp. 1–2.

___. 1991. "Assisted Living: A Housing Type for Older; Frail People: A Philosophy of Care in a Homelike Environment." *Senior Housing News*. Spring. National Association of Home Builders, pp. 1–2.

___; Hamilton, J.; and Yatabe, S. 1991. *Best Practices in Assisted Living: Innovations in Design, Management, and Financing*. Los

Angeles: National Eldercare Institute on Housing and Supportive Services.

___. 1988. "Design for the Semi-Independent Elderly." *Architecture California*. Aug.: v. 10, no. 4. pp. 22–25.

Seip, D. 1990. "The Survival Handbook for Developers of Assisted Living." Boca Raton, Fl.: The Seip Organization.

___. 1989. "First National Assisted Living Industry Survey." *Contemporary Long Term Care* 12:7, pp. 69–70.

___. 1989. "Real Estate Hybrid 'Assisted Living.' A Boon for Elderly." *Providence Journal*. Feb., G–1, G–2.

___. 1989. "Tallying the First National Assisted Living Survey." *Contemporary Long Term Care*. 12: 10, pp. 28, 30, 32–33.

___. 1989. "Free Standing Assisted Living Trends." *Contemporary Long Term Care*. 12; 12, pp. 20, 22–23.

Wilner, M. 1988. Refining the Assisted Living Model to Include Persons of Limited Incomes and Smaller Resident Populations. Portland, Oregon: Milestone Management.

Wilson, K. 1990. "Assisted Living: The Merger of Housing and Long-Term Services." *Long Term Care Advances* 1:4, Duke University Center for the Aging and Human Development, pp. 1–8.

Housing and Health Care for the Frail Elderly

AARP. 1993. *Life Span Design of Residential Environments for the Elderly*. Washington, D.C.: Public Policy Institute.

American Institute of Architects in Cooperation with the American Association of Homes for the Aging. 1992. *Design for Aging, 1992 Review*: Washington D.C.: American Institute of Architects.

Bertram, M. 1989. "A Self-care Project. The Use of Landmarks." *Journal of Gerontological Nursing*, Feb.; 15(2): 6–8.

Brawley, E. 1992. "Alzheimer's Disease: Designing the Physical Environment." *American Journal of Alzheimer's Care and Related Disorders*, Jan.–Feb.; 7(1): 3–8.

Calkins, M. P. 1989. "Designing Cues for Wanderers. Special Needs in Nursing Homes." Architecture, Oct. 78(10): 117–118.

___. 1988. *Designing for Dementia: Planning Environments for the Elderly and Confused*. Owings Mills: National Health Publishing.

Churchmann, A. 1991. Housing for the Elderly and the Meaning of Home. Paper presented at the International Workshop: Home Environment and Physical Space. Corona, Italy. May.

Claygill, J. 1990. Dignity in Dementia. *New Zealand Nursing Journal.* Mar; 83(2): 18–20.

Cohen, U., and Weisman, J. 1991. *Holding on to Home: Designing Environments for People with Dementia.* Baltimore, MD: Johns Hopkins University Press.

Coons, D. H. 1988. "Wandering." *American Journal of Alzheimer's Care and Related Disorders and Research.* Jan.–Feb.: 3(1): 31–36.

Curry, T. J., and Ratliff, B. W. 1973. "The Effect of Nursing Home Size On Resident Isolation and Life Satisfaction." *The Gerontologist.* 13:295–298.

Environmental Design For Aging Research Group. 1992. *Homelike Environments of Dementia Special Care Units.* Ann Arbor, Michigan: National Center on Housing and Living Arrangements for Older Americans.

Fewster, C. 1989. "Making the Patient Feel at Home." *Health Service Journal.* Sept. 21: 99(5169): 1160. pp. 74–86.

Gaskie, M. 1988. "A Little Help: Housing for the Aged." *Architectural Record.* Apr. Vol 196, #4, pp. 98–106.

Gubrium, J. F. 1989. "Domestic Meaning of Institutionalization." *Research on Adulthood and Aging: The Human Science Approach,* ed. T. L. Eugen, 89–106. Albany, NY: University of New York Press.

Hodkinson, E.; McCafferty, F. G.; Scott, J. N., and Stout, R. W. 1988. "Disability and Dependency in Elderly People in Residential and Hospital Care." *Age and Aging.* May: 73 147–154.

Keen, J. 1989. "Interiors: Architecture in the Lives of People With Dementia." *International Journal of Geriatric Psychiatry.* Sept. Oct.: 4(5): 255–277.

Lawton, M. P., et al. 1984. "Architecture for the Mentally Impaired Elderly." *Environment and Behavior.* Nov.: 16(6): 730–757.'

Lindsay, J.; Briggs, K.; Lawes, M.; MacDonald, A.; and Herzberg, J. 1991. "Domus Philosophy: A Contemporary Evaluation of a New Approach to Residential Care for the Demented Elderly." *International Journal of Geriatric Psychiatry.* Oct.: 6(10): 727–736.

Liu, S. 1992. "Searching for a Real Home." Edra 23 Selected Papers Environmental Design Research Association. pp. 47–53.

Marshall, C. and Rossman, G. B. 1989. Designing Qualitative Research. California: Sage Publications.

Morton, D. 1981. "The Age of the Aging." *Progressive Architecture.* Aug.: 59–63.

Namazi, K. L.; Eckert, J. K.; Rosner, T. T.; and Lyon, S. M. 1991. "The

Meaning of Home For the Elderly in Pseudo-Familial Environments." *Adult Residential Care Journal* 5:81–96.

Namazi, K. H., and Johnson, B. D. 1991. "Physical Environmental Cues to Reduce the Problems of Incontinence in Alzheimer's Disease Units." *American Journal of Alzheimer's Care and Related Disorders Research* Nov.–Dec.: 6(6): 22–28.

Peppard, R. N., and McHugh, B. 1988. "Staff Sense of Ownership Key to Special Needs Unit Success." *Provider.* May: 14(5): 30.

Regnier, V. and Pynoos, J. 1994. "The Role of Environmental Design as a Therapeutic Intervention." *Handbook of Mental Health and Aging,* Second ed. J. Birren; B. Sloan; and G. Choen. New York: Academic Press pp. 296–337.

Regnier, V. and Byerts, T. 1983. Applying Research Findings to the Planning and Design of Housing for the Elderly. Housing for a Maturing Population In ed. F. Spink., pp. 24–49. Washington, Urban Land Institute.

Rovins, G. 1994. "Exploring the Environmental Effectiveness of Normalization Principles for Older Persons With Developmental Disabilities." Adult Residential Care Journal. J 38(2), pp. 16–20.

Special Committee on Aging. 1989. Aging America: Trends and Projections Series 101E. Washington D.C.: U.S. Government Printing Office.

Strieb, G. 1983. "The Frail Elderly: Research Dilemmas and Research Opportunities." *The Gerontologist,* 3, pp. 40–44.

U.S. Senate Subcommittee on Aging. 1991. *Aging America.* Washington, D.C.

Williams, C. C. 1989. "The Experience of Long Term Care in the Future." *Journal of Gerontological Social Work* 14: 1–2, 3–18.

House and Home

Archer, W. 1981. "House as Archetype." *Architectural Review* v. 170, no. 105, pp. 137–168.

Altman, I., and Werner, C. eds. 1985. "Home Environments." Vols. 1 and 2, *Human Behavior and Environment: Advances in Theory and Research.* New York: Plenum Press.

Cooper-Marcus, C. 1974. *House as a Symbol of Self.* Berkeley, California: University of California Berkeley Press.

Cooper-Marcus, C. and Sarkissan, W. 1986. *Housing as if People Mattered.* Berkeley, California: University of California Berkeley Press.

Heidegger, M.S. 154. *Ans der Erfahrung des Denkens,* Pfulungen, English Translation: "Building, Dwelling, Thinking" in Poetry, Language, Thought.

Holl, S. 1982. *Rural and Urban House Types.* Pamphlet Architecture series New Haven, Connecticut.

Jackson, K. 1985. *Crabgrass Frontier,* New York: Oxford University Press.

Joselit, D. 1984. "The Post-War House." *Arts and Architecture* v.3, no. 3. pp. 23–29.

McAllister, V. 1984. *A Field Guide to the American House.* New York: Alfred Knopf.

Metre, J. 1983. "Thoughts on Symbols in the Suburbs." *Metropolis.* June: v.2, no. 10. pp. 31–37.

Murphy, J. 1987. "The Image of the House." *Progressive Architecture.* Dec.; v. 68, no. 13, pp. 59–107.

Norberg-Schulz, C. 1985. *The Concept of Dwelling.* New York: Rizolli.

Rapoport, A. 1967. *House Form and Culture.* Englewood: New Jersey: Prentice-Hall.

Roberts, W. 1987. "The Comfortable House: North American Suburban Architecture 1890–1930." *Winterthur Portfolio* v.22, no. 4., pp. 58–62.

Rowe, P. 1991. *Making a Middle Landscape,* Cambridge, Massachusetts: MIT Press.

Rybczinski, W. 1986. *Home: A Short History of an Idea.* New York: Viking Penguin.

Scott-Brown, D. 1977. "Suburban Space, Scale, and Symbols." *Learning From Levittown.* New Haven, Connecticut: Yale University Press.

Stern, R. 1981. *The Anglo American Suburb.* London, England: AD Profile.

Stillgoe, J. 1988. *Borderland.* New Haven, Connecticut: Yale University Press.

Taylor, L. 1982. *Housing: Symbol, Structure and Site.* New York: Cooper-Hewitt Museum.

Thiis-Evensen, T. 1989. *Archetypes in Architecture.* Norwegian Press.

Vaughan, T. and Guest-Ferriday, V. eds. 1974. *Space Style and Structure: Building in N.W. America.* Portland, Oregon: Oregon Historical Society.

APPENDIX B

ANNOTATED BIBLIOGRAPHY

1) AARP. 1993. *Assisted Living In the U.S.: A New Paradigm for Residential Care for Frail Older Persons.*

- *Cost-effectiveness of assisted living*
- *National service and environmental conditions/components*
- *Progressive government roles*
- *Oregon's assisted living program*

Rosalie Kane and Keren Brown Wilson coauthor this comprehensive national overview of current trends, issues, and conditions in assisted living. Perspectives of managers and administrators of assisted living facilities, as well as developers, researchers, experts, and regulators are presented in an effort to outline potential conflicts, strengths, weaknesses, and future directions in this rapidly growing industry. A focused study of pioneering assisted living programs in Oregon is included. Conclusions discussed include the relative lower costs of assisted living versus nursing home environments, opportunities for environment enhancements (such as private rooms, baths, kitchenettes, and homelike environments), and approaches to offsetting the cost of such, the ability of Assisted Living to meet and adapt to changing resident needs, the efficiency of flexible and responsive staffing patterns, and potential supportive roles of government agencies.

2) Bowe, J. 1993 *Medicaid Takes the Plunge into Assisted Living.*

- *Medicaid reimbursement trends*
- *Responsibility sharing for elderly housing/healthcare*
- *Potential shifts in nursing home position*

An interview of Richard Ladd, formerly with the Oregon Department of Human Resources (and instrumental in developing the state's assisted living program), and Keren Brown Wilson, of Concepts in Community Living (among the first of Oregon's developers to initiate projects under the waiver program) is conducted by Bowe. Ladd and Wilson discuss the economic and therapeutic advantages of assisted living and the expanding of Medicaid funding to it, and the changes in elderly housing and health care philosophy such implies.

3) Churchmann, A. 1991. *Housing for the Elderly and the Meaning of Home.*

- *Independence versus dependence*
- *Private rooms versus no provision for privacy*

An analysis of the possible meanings of "home" for elderly residents living in independent housing, sheltered housing (CCRC), and nursing homes is carried out through the categorization of meanings into four groups—lifestyle/setting, security, control, and expressive/symbolic. Churchman then rated the three housing types in terms of how well they afford the possible meanings to the resident. Independent housing rated high in all categories of meaning, with the exception of "medical support." Sheltered housing rated relatively high when separate, single-occupancy apartments are provided, but low when there are only shared spaces. Nursing homes rated low on all terms/meanings excepting actual physical shelter and "basic needs."

4) Cohen, U., and Weisman, J. 1991. *Holding on to Home: Designing Environments for People with Dementia.*

- *Alzheimer's disease-specific issues*
- *Residential quality/noninstitutional quality*
- *Behavior-service-socialization-environment integration*

Cohen and Weisman develop planning and design guidelines which integrate the special needs of people with Alzheimer's disease in terms of social, behavioral, and organizational dimensions with architectural design that is supportive of these needs and embraces residential character. The guidelines are outlined in terms of "General Attributes of the Environment," "Overall Building Organization," and "Activity Areas." Each section links design concepts with therapeutic goals and related issues regarding people with dementia.

5) Contemporary Long Term Care. 1993. *Bolder Design Solutions Needed.*

- *Complete residential environment*
- *Decentralization of services and activity places*
- *Residential materiality*

An interview of architects Victor Regnier, David Hoglund, and developer and Assisted Living Facilities Association of America (ALFAA) president Paul Klausson suggests directions and considerations for design solutions to assisted living facilities. Issues discussed include the decentralization of services and activity spaces; interior residential spatial quality and materiality; and a more meaningful understanding and response to the frail elderly resident.

6) Cooper-Marcus, C. 1974. *House as a Symbol of Self.*

- *House–self*
- *House–universe*

Cooper-Marcus links house with both our image of the universe (macrocosm) and our image of our self (microcosm). Through a Jung-based approach of the relationship of archetype-symbol-artifact, the symbolic content of the public face of the house (our image we wish to reflect to society) and the interior realm (our valued self-image) is explored.

7) Hoglund, D. 1985. *Housing for the Elderly: Privacy and Independence in Environments for the Aging.*

- *Residential character*
- *Integration with community*
- *Privacy affordance*
- *Independence fostering*

European case studies of environments for housing and caring for the elderly are used as a basis for underscoring the importance of privacy and independence. Strengths and weaknesses of each case are discussed, including issues such as integration with the community; establishment of residential character; purposeful and useful shared spaces; service delivery that is both adequately supportive and independence fostering; appropriate layering, cueing, affordance of privacy; and responsiveness to changing needs and evolving abilities/disabilities.

8) Kane, R., Illuston, L., and Nyman, J. 1990. *Meshing Services with Housing: Lessons From Adult Foster Care and Assisted Living in Oregon.*

- *Defining assisted living*
- *Oregon's assisted living program*
- *Housing-service integration*

The newly evolving housing type of assisted living is studied in terms of its organizational, physical, economic, and service-delivery structures in an effort to describe its current successes and failures, and the applicability of Oregon's pioneering Assisted Living support program to other states and contexts. Assisted Living is seen as an option providing more therapeutic and humane housing and health care environments for those who would otherwise most likely be placed in a nursing home.

9) Kalymun, M. 1990. *"Toward a Definition of Assisted Living." In Optimizing Housing for the Elderly: Homes Not Houses, ed. L. Pastalan.*

- *Importance of residential character*
- *Comprehensive and responsive services*
- *Definition of assisted living*
- *Placement of assisted living in housing/health care continuum*

Ten southeastern Florida assisted living facilities are studied in an effort to identify the concepts and philosophies of Assisted Living by the physical characteristics of the setting, services offered, and the functional competence of the residents, and to ascertain its position within the elderly housing/health care continuum. Primary conclusions include the importance of homelike quality and the nature of comprehensive, individualized, intense, and responsive services.

10) Miller, J. A. and Patten, T. M. 1991. "Concepts in Community Living Assisted Living Program. Portland, Oregon." *In Community-Based Long Term Care: Innovative Models.*

- *Resident choice/autonomy/control*
- *Individualized services*
- *Homelike quality*
- *Privacy*

This case study of Concepts in Community Living, a Portland-based development firm specializing in Assisted Living, describes the philosophy and principles that guide this progressive and successful firm. Individuality and independence form the foundation of their integrative housing-health care model. Important principles include "a place of ones own"—private rooms; common space; embracing homelike quality; tailoring services to individual and changing needs; sharing of the responsibility for care and wellness; and resident empowerment.

11) Rapoport, A. 1967. *House Form and Culture*

- *Symbolic content of house*
- *Cultural and behavioral factors*
- *House within community*

Rapoport's discussion springs from a hypothesis that house form is the consequence of a broad range of sociocultural factors—including a population's vision of the ideal life and understanding of the universe and one's place within it; and secondary factors—including climatic conditions, methods of construction, technology and available materials. Rapoport concludes that man builds not only to control his physical environment, but equally his social/cultural/behavioral environment as well. "House" is discussed in terms of its place as an integral member of a community, *affecting* community behavior and form as well as being *affected by* it.

12) Rowe, P. 1991. *Making a Middle Landscape*

- *Suburban symbolism*
- *American ideals after World War II*

Suburban growth, forms, and organizations are discussed in terms of their physical structure and symbolic content. The impact of the automobile on the form of shared space (once urban, now suburban), neighborhood space, and the relationship of private space to communal space are seen as primary issues.

13) Regnier, V. 1994. *Assisted Living Housing for the Elderly: Design Innovations from the United States and Europe.*

- *European philosophy/approach/innovation*
- *Noninstitutional environments*
- *Connections to community and family*
- *Landscape issues*

Regnier discusses issues regarding housing for the frail elderly, founded on this population's special needs, and then outlines management and design directives addressing these needs. Fifteen "Enrichment Themes" are drawn, including stretching regulations, therapeutic design, inviting the family, serving the broader community, landscape design, dwelling unit features, and residential imagery. These are illustrated through case studies of innovative models of assisted living facilities in northern Europe and the United States.

14) Regnier, V., Hamilton, J., and Yatabe, S. 1991. *Best Practices in Assisted Living: Innovations in Design, Management, and Financing.*

- *Defining assisted living*
- *Residential character*
- *Links to community*
- *Management of assisted living*
- *Financing assisted living*

Regnier discusses general design, organizational and economic issues of Assisted Living through case-study analysis of exemplary facilities in the United States. Key design issues identified include creating residential character; clustering units to articulate mass; including features of homes in apartments (such as kitchen, storage closets, articulated bays, etc.); clarity of spatial organization and hierarchy; consideration of resident difficulties with grasp and manipulation; deinstitutionalization of corridors; and linkages to the community.

15) Scott-Brown, W. 1977. "Suburban Space Scale and Symbols." in *Learning From Levittown*.

- *Suburban symbolism*
- *Public facade*

An architectural analysis of suburbia of the 1970s is conducted in an effort to understand the meaning and symbolism behind its architecture. Scott-Brown describes suburbia as a place just as rich in symbolism as past urban living environments. The artifacts used to note the symbols have changed, but the need and use of signs to represent issues of territoriality, control, privacy, ownership, and status remain constant.

APPENDIX C

REFERENCES AND SOURCES OF FURTHER INFORMATION

Alzheimer's Association
1334 G Street N.W., Suite 500
Washington, D.C. 20005

American Association of Homes for the Aging
901 E Street N.W., Suite 500
Washington, D.C. 20004-2037

American Association of Retired Persons
601 E Street N.W.
Washington, D.C. 20049

American Society for Hospital Engineering of the American Hospital Association
840 N. Lake Shore Drive—8W
Chicago, IL 60611

American Institute of Architects
1735 New York Avenue, N.W.
Washington, D.C. 20086

American Society of Aging
833 Market Street
San Francisco, CA 94103

Assisted Living Facilities Association of America
Association Headquarters
9401 Lee Highway, 3rd Floor
Fairfax, VA 22031

Concepts in Community Living
10570 S.E. Washington Street, Suite 210
Portland, OR 97216

Institute on Aging and Environment
University of Wisconsin/Milwaukee
School of Architecture and Urban Planning
P.O. Box 413
Milwaukee, WI 53201

Institute for Health Service Research
University of Minnesota
420 Delaware Street S.E.
Box 729
Minneapolis, MN 55455

National Association of State Units on Aging
2003 K Street N.W., Suite 304
Washington, D.C. 20006

APPENDIX D

APPROACH AND METHOD OF STUDY

The monograph is the result of two years of research and analysis focused on the architectural design of assisted living facilities. Two studies were conducted during this period. The first was a preliminary investigation of the definition, issues, resident needs and problems of Assisted Living. The second was an in-depth research and design project funded by a Graduate Fellowship in Health Facility Planning and Design granted by the American Hospital Association and the American Institute of Architects, and two Fellowships from the Institute on Aging and Environment of the School of Architecture and Urban Planning at the University of Wisconsin at Milwaukee.

The first step in this work was to gain an informed understanding of the important and definitive characteristics and qualities of Assisted Living. Also important to this phase of the work was to ascertain if the hypothesized problem (lack of meaningful and successful interpretation of home) was indeed significant and, if it was, what could be the cause of the problem.

The first study involved a preliminary literature review; voluntary, informal, on-site interviews with 19 residents and nine staff members and administrators at six assisted living facilities in the Milwaukee, Wisconsin area; and ten telephone interviews with noted experts in Assisted Living. The paper which was the product of this study developed a working definition of Assisted Living, resident needs and problems assessment, and outlined current problems and recommendations for further study.

The recommendations of areas for further study include:

1. The decentralization of services
2. Appropriate accessibility standards for frail elderly
3. Ways and means of more community-integrated assisted living solutions
4. Appropriate building codes and regulation
5. The definition and exploration of the meaning of "homelike character"

The second study focused on exploring the meaning and issues of "homelike character." This involved an in-depth analysis of the concepts and architectural realizations of home and the derivation of architectural design considerations for integrating homelike character in assisted living environments.

This more-intensive study included a comprehensive review of current literature on assisted living and the architecture of home; 16 case studies of exemplary assisted living facilities nationwide; interviews of 43 residents and 22 staff members and administrators within these facilities; telephone interviews of 12 family members of assisted living residents; and periodic consultation with noted experts in Assisted Living throughout the development of the project.

Case-study facilities were selected through literature review and recommendation by experts in the field. The case-study procedure involved on-site tours and photographing of each facility; collection of architectural plans/drawings and promotional materials for analysis that included descriptions of services, clientele, and costs; and on-site behavioral and environmental observations and notation. Below is a list of participating assisted living facilities:

Alexian Village
Milwaukee, Wisconsin

Annie Maxim House
Rochester, Massachusetts

Brighton Gardens
Virginia Beach, Virginia

Captain Eldridge Congregate Care
Hyannis, Massachusetts

Corrine Dolan Center
Chardon, Ohio

Elder Homestead
Minnetonka, Minnesota

Lincolnia Senior Center
Fairfax, Virginia

Rackleff House
Canby, Oregon

Regency Park
Portland, Oregon

Rosewood Estates
Roseville, Minnesota

Sunrise Retirement Home of Arlington
Arlington, Virginia

Sunrise Retirement Home of Falls Church
Falls Church, Virginia

Sunrise Retirement Home Of Mercer Island
Seattle, Washington

Sunrise at Queen Anne
Seattle, Washington

Villa St. Francis
Milwaukee, Wisconsin

Woodside Place
Oakmont, Pennsylvania

The intention of the resident interviews was to gain an understanding of the needs and desires of the residents with regard to assistance, and preferred quality and characteristics of the assisted living environments. An interview map was developed to guide questions and discussions in an effort to cover a broad range of behavioral and environmental issues without limiting or precluding responses, and to establish and maintain an informal and comfortable interview milieu. The acknowledgment with this decision was that a highly empirical data collection instrument and tabulation system that meaningfully explored the depth and range of these issues was beyond the reasonable scope, intent, and resources of this project. Interviews were conducted voluntarily, on-site, either in resident's apartments or in a shared space within the facility. Discussion formats ranged from one-on-one interviews to discussion groups of two to six residents. Interviews were recorded and transcriptions edited to eliminate discussion off-topic or irrelevant to the project's area of study.

Staff and administrator interviews were conducted to ascertain the issues and problems they considered important, the priority they attached to creating homelike character, and how they attempted to embrace this character if they felt it was of value. All these interviews were conducted one-to-one in private office/work spaces, recorded and similarly transcribed.

Interviews with experts began with discussions of the general issues and problems currently facing assisted living facilities, and subsequent discussions increasingly focused on the architectural component of Assisted Living and homelike character, and on critique of the process and content of this monograph. Below is a list of participating assisted living and elderly housing/health care expert consultants:

Ms. Margaret Calkins
Fellow, Institute on Aging and Environment
University of Wisconsin/Milwaukee

Mr. Uriel Cohen
Director, Institute on Aging and Environment
University of Wisconsin/Milwaukee

Mr. David Hoglund
Perkins Eastman and Partners, Architects
New York, New York

Ms. Mary Kalymun
Department of Human Development, Counseling and Family Studies
University of Rhode Island
Kingston, Rhode Island

Ms. Rosalie Kane
Institute for Health Service Research
University of Minnesota
Minneapolis, Minnesota

Mr. Paul Klaasson
Assisted Living Facilities Association of America and Sunrise Retirement Homes
Fairfax, Virginia

Mr. Barry Korobkin
Korobkin Associates, Architects
Somerville, Massachusetts

Mr. Victor Regnier
Dean, Department of Architecture and Urban Planning, and Andrus Gerontology Center
University of Southern California
Los Angeles, California

Mr. David Seip
The Seip Group
Boca Raton, Florida

Mr. Gerald Weisman
Institute on Aging and Environment
University of Wisconsin/Milwaukee

Ms. Keren Brown-Wilson
Concepts in Community Living
Portland, Oregon

Telephone interviews of family members were focused on the questions of what conditions, problems, or frailties led to their loved ones (e.g., parent) move into an assisted living facility, what were they seeking in an environment/service, how important (if at all) was it for the environment to be homelike, and what factors led to the decision of placement where their loved one now resides.

This information was gathered and analyzed using admittingly quasi-scientific, qualitative methods. The intent was to gain a breadth and richness of information that would best serve as a background from which to sound ideas.

The second phase of this work involved a series of analyses of the concepts and supporting architecture of "home." Literature review provided much of the conceptual framework, and images of home were the springboard for discussion and analysis.

It was decided that in order to understand how to make an environment homelike, one had to study *home,* and not other presumably "homelike" environments. This was perhaps a critical missing link in current literature on Assisted Living. Researchers were promoting homelike environments, yet none were studying *home.*

It was also decided to study (and provide as illustrations in this work) primarily only the better works of architecture. One of the biggest problems with current literature on assisted living environments is that most of the images used are either uninspiring, or stereotypical to elderly. It is as if it is assumed that as one ages, one loses sensibility to refinement and beauty, and prefers a "Tudor Box" to a refined work of architecture. This lack of quality architectural images in published works on this subject also proliferates the misunderstanding that assisted living environments are, or should be, hospital-like, nouveau Victorian, or hotel-like. This issue is at the root of the decision to favor images of beautiful residential architecture (not necessarily limited to assisted living environments), whose ideas and inspirations could be applied to assisted living environments.

The last phase of this work was to derive architectural design considerations that respond to the characteristics of "home" and the needs of assisted living residents.

INDEX

Ability-enhancing approach, 6, 102
Accessibility
  in Assisted Living, 16
  impediments to, 81
  manipulation of, 75
Activity
  functional ability and, 105
  homelike, 103
  levels of participation in, 106
  personal choice in, 102–103
  previewing, 91–92
Activity kitchens, 97–98
  at Corvallis Assisted Living, 123, 131
  at Rosewood Estates, 119
"Activity rooms," 87, 95
Adaptability, in Assisted Living, 16
Aging, xi. *See also* Elderly population
  philosophy of, 80
Alcoves, 80
  for dining, 90
  sitting, 94
Alzheimer's disease, 8, 82. *See also* Cognitive impairment
Amenities, adaptable, 75
American Hospital Association, x, 149
American Institute of Architects, x, 149
Annie Maxim House, 20, 45
  fireplace at, 48
  laundry room at, 98
  library at, 96
  main living room at, 71
Apartment clusters, 58
Apartment complexes, articulated, 58
Apartment controls
  adjustable, 79
  at Corvallis Assisted Living, 128
  at Rosewood Estates, 116
Apartment doors, locking, 79
Apartment plans, types of, 22

Apartments, 43. *See also* Private apartments
  at Corvallis Assisted Living, 125
  at Rosewood Estates, 114
Architectural cues, redundant, 70
Architectural design considerations, 39–100
  structure of, 40
Architectural plans, types of, 20–21
Architectural program, 18
  sample, 19
Architecture
  quality of life and, ix
  as the tone of environment, 25
Articulation
  intimacy and, 46
  of mass and form, 57–59
  single-level, 48
Assistance level, 4
  as-needed basis for, 105
  choice in, 102
Assistance needs
  higher, 7–8
  lower, 4, 7
  traditional responses to, 8–13
Assisted Living, x, xi, xii
  advantages of, 23–24
  architectural design considerations for, 39–100
  architectural design of, 25–26
  behavioral considerations for, 101–106
  as a building type, 17–23
  components of, 14–15
  defined, 3–24
  evolution of, 13–14
  licensure of, 22
  needs and problems driving, 3–4
  obstacles to, 28–29
  philosophies and approaches in, 16–17, 101–103
  as a social phenomenon, 15–17
Assisted Living facilities, 14
  architectural program for, 19

government regulation of, 22–23
  location of, 17–18
Assisted transfers, 10, 12
Atrium, triangular, 66
Autonomy
  in Assisted Living, 16
  maximizing, 104
  in nursing homes, 12

Back entry system, 67
Backyard realm, 64–65
  at Corvallis Assisted Living, 126
  at Rosewood Estates, 114
  workshop-centered, 88
Balconies, 77
Bathing, 86–87
  at Corvallis Assisted Living, 130
  at Rosewood Estates, 117
Bathrooms, 81, 82
Bathtubs, side-entry, 86
Bedridden elderly, 6
Behavioral considerations, 101–106
Behavioral cueing, 8, 105–106
Berkowitz-Odgis House, 74
Board and care homes, 11–12
  regulations for, 22
Boundaries, clarifying, 59
Brummett, William, 19, 44, 54, 59, 64, 68
BRW Elness, Associates, 20, 22, 46, 56, 67
Building codes, 22, 23
Building Dwelling Thinking (Heidegger), 27
Building envelope, 75–76
  at Corvallis Assisted Living, 127–128
  at Rosewood Estates, 115
Building organization, 69
Buildings, 17–23
  organization of, 18, 69
  resident contact with, 49
  unarticulated, 57

Cafe, public, 52
Caregivers, shared household with, 8–10,
Caregiving approach, 102
Caregiving staff, 28–29
  supporting, 106
Care receivers, empowerment of, 11
Case-by-case service delivery, 15
Casual previews, 91–92
  at Corvallis Assisted Living, 130
  at Rosewood Estates, 118
Center/origin concept, 37
  design considerations for, 56–59
Central-entry architectural plan, 20
Chair rails, integrated, 82
Charnley House, 92
Chilless-Nielsen Architects, 21, 45, 73
Choice, 6
  in Assisted Living, 16
  of desired services, 17
  in nursing homes, 12
Choice/opportunity concept, 37

design considerations for, 87–100
Christenson-Puopolo, Bethany, 46
Circulation routes, 72–73
  at Corvallis Assisted Living, 127
  rest spots along, 93, 94
  at Rosewood Estates, 115
Clark & Meneffee, 69, 95
Clustered-apartment architectural plan, 21
Coastal house, 41
Cognitive impairment, 5, 8
  circulation routes and, 72–73
  outdoor space and, 64
  wayfinding and, 43, 44, 69
Comatose states, 6
Commercial connections, 17
Commercial/public components, 76
Community, 17
  participation in, 24, 103, 105
Community-engaging space, 50
Community-integrated sites, 51–52
  at Corvallis Assisted Living, 122
  at Rosewood Estates, 113
Community interaction, 52–53
  at Corvallis Assisted Living, 122–123
  at Rosewood Estates, 113
Competence and Environmental Press Theory, 13–14
"Concept of Dwelling, The" (Norberg-Schultz), 35
Concepts of home, defined, 33–36
Confused states, 7. *See also* Cognitive impairment
Congruence Model of Person Environment Interaction, 13–14
Connectedness/belonging concept, 36
  design considerations for, 49–56
Consistency, maintaining, 105
Construction costs, 23
Contemporary housing, 35
Continuing Care Retirement Community (CCRC), 17, 18
Continuity, maintaining, 105
Continuum of care model, 9
  with Assisted Living, 15
Control, 6
  in Assisted Living, 16
  maximizing, 104
  in nursing homes, 12
Control/autonomy concept, 37
  design considerations for, 74–75
Cooper-Marcus, Clare, 27, 34, 41
Corner details, 46
Corridors, 44–47
  at Corvallis Assisted Living, 121
  at Rosewood Estates, 110
Corvallis Assisted Living, 19, 65, 120–132
  project overview of, 120
Costs
  of Assisted Living, 14, 23
  of board and care homes, 12
  of in-home health services, 11
  of nursing homes, 13

in shared households, 10
Courtyards, 21, 64, 65
  at Corvallis Assisted Living, 122
  fountain-centered, 89
  pavilion-centered, 88
Craft activity, 97
Croffead House, 69, 95
Custodial care approach, xii

Daily living activities of, 4, 6
  philosophy and approaches to, 102
Debilitating conditions, 82
Decision making, in Assisted Living, 16
Deck areas, 65, 66, 77
Delivery personnel, 66–67. *See also* Modified delivery space and system
Dementia, 7. *See also* Alzheimer's disease; Cognitive impairment
Dependent relationships, 13, 28
Design, 33–38
  clarity and redundancy in, 69–71
Detail, texture and scale of, 46–49
Dignity, 6
  in Assisted Living, 16
  during bathing, 86
  in nursing homes, 12
Dining, 89–91
  at Corvallis Assisted Living, 130
  at Rosewood Estates, 118
Disabilities, categories of, 5–7
Disorientation, 7
Display cases, 43, 44
Dogtrot house, 68
Door handles, 83
Doors, 79, 100
Double-loaded corridors, 45

Easy adaptability, defined, 80
Economies of scale, 24
Edge layers, 77
Educational exchanges, providing, 106
Elder Homestead, 67
Elderly housing, 36
  solutions to, 132–133
Elderly Housing Cooperative, 64
Elderly population, xi. *See also* Frail elderly
  housing demand by, 13
  partially dependent, 4
Emotional needs, 4, 103
Entries, 42–44
  at Corvallis Assisted Living, 121, 127
  orienting, 71–72
  at Rosewood Estates, 110, 115
Entry alcove, 43
Entry stairs, 49
Environmental conditions, control of, 74
Environmental controls, 79
Environmental familiarity, 16
Environments, 26. *See also* Homelike character
  homelike, 103
  responsive, 81

European Assisted Living prototypes, 53
Evaluation, of service needs, 17
Exercise, 17, 73. *See also* Circulation routes
Exterior rooms, 88–89
  at Corvallis Assisted Living, 130
  at Rosewood Estates, 117–118

Facilities
  as community members, 53
  as residents' households, 104
Familiarity/order concept, 37
  design considerations for, 67–73
Family involvement, promoting, 105
Farmhouse pattern, 50
Federal funding
  of assisted living facilities, 22
  for board and care homes, 12
  for nursing homes, 13
Finish materials, exterior and interior, 26
Fireplace, 95
  at Annie Maxim House, 48
Fixtures, 47
  locating, 82
Form, 57–59
  at Corvallis Assisted Living, 124–125
  at Rosewood Estates, 114
For-profit elderly housing, 15
Frail elderly, ix–x
  increasing numbers of, xi
  quality of life for, 15
Freestanding facilities, 17–18
French doors, 63
Functional ability, supporting, 105
Functional impairment, categories of, 5–7
Furnishings, built-in, 47

Garage components, 67
Gardens, private, 76
Gardening, purposeful, 88
Gathering space, central, 70. *See also* Group living
Gerontology-environment studies, xii
Glessner House, 63, 72
  dining room at, 90
  library at, 87
Goods, delivery of, 66–67
Government regulation, 12
  of assisted living facilities, 22–23
Government subsidies. *See* Federal funding
Graves Residence, 49
Greenhouse yards, 88
Grooming, cueing and assistance with, 6
Group activity spaces, 52
Group living, 28
  hospital model of, 35–36

Handicap accessibility, 10. *See also* Wheelchair accessibility
Handrails, 94
Hardware, 82–83
  at Corvallis Assisted Living, 128

at Rosewood Estates, 116
Health care options, xi–xii
Heidegger, Martin, 26–27, 35
Hertzberger, Herman, 75, 94
History, promoting a sense of, 105
Holistic views, xii
Home, xii–xiii
　architectural essence of, 27–28
　Assisted Living contradictions to, 28–29
　meaning and symbolism of, 34–35, 38
Home Concept Interpretation Diagram, 34
Homelike character, x, 10
　attempts at, 26
　of board and care homes, 11–12
　of buildings, 18–21
　creating, 27–28
　versus durability, 48
　integrating, 28–29
　in nursing homes, 13
　in shared households, 10
Homelike environments, xii, 14, 25
Homelike tasks, engagement in, 97–98
House, self-image and, 35
House as a Symbol of Self (Cooper-Marcus), 27
Household management, problems with, 4
Housing complexes, arrangement of, 50
Housing/health care facilities, xi–xiii
　European, 14
Hygiene, cueing and assistance with, 6

Ice cream parlor, 53
Identification, 35
　concepts emerging from, 36, 38
　design considerations for, 41–56
Identity, 13
　sense of wellness and, 26–27
Impairment, environmental comprehension and, 61. See also Cognitive impairment
Incontinence, 5, 8. See also Toilet rooms
Independence, 6
　in Assisted Living, 16
　inspiring, 104
Information gathering, resources for, 147–148
In-home health services, 10–11
Institutional behaviors, 29
Institutional environments, humanizing, 26, 46
Institutional materials, 47
Institute on Aging and Environment, x, 149
Integration, 28–29
　behavioral strategies for, 103–106
Isolation, combatting, 51
Israel, Frank, 62, 83

Jung, Carl, 33

Keys, personal, 55
Kitchenettes, 78–79
　at Corvallis Assisted Living, 128
　at Rosewood Estates, 115
Kitchens. See Activity kitchens
Korobkin, Barry, 20, 45
Krier, Rob, 49

Landmarks, 70
　in corridor systems, 45–46
Laundry, 98–99
　at Corvallis Assisted Living, 131
　at Rosewood Estates, 119
Lawns, as site edges, 60
Layering, 52–53
　of interior and exterior spaces, 76
Lever hardware, 82
Licensed caregivers, 10–11
Lighting, 47
　incandescent, 85, 86
Living areas, 62–63
　at Corvallis Assisted Living, 125–126
　at Rosewood Estates, 114
Living room activity spaces, 94–96
　at Corvallis Assisted Living, 131
　at Rosewood Estates, 118
Locks, personal, 55
Log cabin, 57
Loved ones, shared household with, 8–10
Lower-income residents, subsidies for, 22–23
　See also Federal funding

Machado Silvetti and Associates, 43
Madeline House, 93
Mailbox events, 53–55
　at Corvallis Assisted Living, 124
　at Rosewood Estates, 113
Mason, Ron, 57
Mass, 57–59
　at Corvallis Assisted Living, 124–125
　at Rosewood Estates, 114
Material quality, 47–48
　at Corvallis Assisted Living, 121
　at Rosewood Estates, 111
Materials, exterior, 47
Meals, 5–6, 17, 78, 90. See also Dining
Medicaid Waiver Act (Oregon), 22–23
Medical advancements, xi
Medical alert services, 17
Medical assistance, 17
Medicare system, 13
Medication, assistance with, 6, 17
Meeting halls, 52. See also Group living
Mercer Island, 96, 97
Merrill, Scott, 51
Michael Graves, Architects, 49
Mobility impairment, 5, 7–8, 52, 81–82
　resting spots and, 93–94
Modified delivery place and system, 66–67
　at Corvallis Assisted Living, 126
　at Rosewood Estates, 115
"Mud room," 67
Multidimensional continuum of care, 9, 15
Multistory facilities, 92–93

Nahum House, 68
National Fellowship for Research and Design of Healthcare Facilities, x
Needs, adaptability to changes in, 80–81, 104, 116, 128

Noninstitutional environments, 14
Norberg-Schultz, Christian, 35
Normalcy, 6–7
  maintaining, 15
Nursing care, financial burden of, 14
Nursing homes, x, 12–13
  operational environments in, 29
  psychological effects of, 13

Oak Park Studio (Wright), 71
Observation areas, 84–85
  at Corvallis Assisted Living, 129
  at Rosewood Estates, 117
Occupational therapy, 53
Office connections, 99–100
  at Corvallis Assisted Living, 132
  at Rosewood Estates, 119
Operating costs, decrease in, 23
Operational environment, flexibility of, 8
Order, 69–71
  at Corvallis Assisted Living, 126–127
  at Rosewood Estates, 115
Orientation, 35, 36–37, 38
  design considerations for, 56–73
  heightening, 104
Outdoor activity, 64–65, 89
  semi-private, 74
Outdoor space, 76–77
  at Corvallis Assisted Living, 128
  at Rosewood Estates, 115
"Overservicing," 13

Parking, 55–56
  at Corvallis Assisted Living, 124
  at Rosewood Estates, 113
Partially dependent elderly, 4
Participation levels, choosing, 106
Pedestrian walkways, houses fronting, 51
Perkins Eastman Architects, 21
Personal care, 17
Personal items, placement of, 42–44
Physical (functional) needs, 4
Physical barriers, 11
Physical environment, 17–23. *See also* Homelike character
  relationship to behavior, 26
  therapeutic potential of, 13–14
  unspecific, 88
Physical frailty, 7. *See also* Frail elderly
Physical limitations, of caregivers, 10
Physical obstacles, eliminating, 83
Physical well-being, considering, 29
Plumbing fixtures, 47
Pocket doors, 63
Pool rooms, 96
Porches, 77
  semi-transparent, 51
  transparent, 59
Previewing objects, 91–92
Privacy, 6, 16, 28, 104
  in assistance matters, 102
  during bathing, 86
Privacy/territoriality concept, 37
  design considerations for, 59–67
Private apartments, 22, 60–61
  at Corvallis Assisted Living, 125
  at Rosewood Estates, 114
"Private lounges," 61
Private/public interface, control of, 59
Private space, environmental cues for, 43
Protective oversight, 5, 7, 11, 17
Psychological well-being, 4, 103
Public places, including, 52

Qualification, 35
  concepts emerging from, 37, 38
Quality of life, ix, 15

Rackleff House, 21, 73, 94
Reception areas, 84–85
  at Corvallis Assisted Living, 129
  at Rosewood Estates, 117
Regency Park, 88
Registered caregivers, 10–11
Regulation/code analysts, 23
Regulations, 23–24
  challenging, 83–84, 117, 129
Resident apartments, 22. *See also* Apartments
Resident-community interaction, stimulating, 52
Resident needs, responses to, 28
Resident profiles, 7–8
Residents, 3–7
  effects of relocating, 51
  perceptions of Assisted Living, 25, 26
Resident-staff interaction, 99–100
Rest spots, 75, 93–94
  at Corvallis Assisted Living, 130
  at Rosewood Estates, 118
Richardson, H. H., 63, 87
Robert A. M. Stearn, Architects, 41, 50
Roof form, articulated, 58
Rooms, 80. *See also* Exterior rooms
  homelike themes for, 95–96
Roseville, sunroom at, 95
Rosewood Estates, 20, 22, 110–119
  dining room at, 90
  ground floor plan of, 111
  parking at, 56
  project overview of, 110
  service entry at, 67
Roto Architects, 91
Routine, individuality in, 54
Rowe, Colin, xiii

Safety standards, problems with, 29
Scale, 48–50
  at Corvallis Assisted Living, 122
  at Rosewood Estates, 112
Seaside house, 49
Security, 5

in Assisted Living, 16, 17
  ensuring, 104
Security/safety concept, 37
  design considerations for, 74–75
Self, home as a symbol of, 41
Self-maintenance, 16
Self-protection/self-symbol concept, 36
  design considerations for, 41–46
Semi-dependent residents, 3
Senate Subcommittee on Aging Report, xi
Sensory impairments, 5, 8
Service delivery, 14–15, 25, 101–103
Service exchanges, providing, 106
Service model, 12
Service needs, dynamic nature of, 16–17
Services
  in Assisted Living, 16–17, 23
  in board and care homes, 11
  of in-home health services, 10–11
  of nursing homes, 12–13
  in shared households, 10
Service spaces, 18
Shared household option, 8–10
Shared spaces, 96–97
  at Corvallis Assisted Living, 131
  at Rosewood Estates, 118
Single-loaded wings architectural plan, 20
Single-occupancy apartments, 60–61
Sites, 51–52
  community-integrated, 113
Sitting space, corridor, 45
Sleeping areas, 62–63
  at Corvallis Assisted Living, 125–126
  at Rosewood Estates, 114
Social enrichment, philosophy and approaches to, 102–103
Social interaction, 17, 106. *See also* Mailbox events
  in the backyard realm, 65
  dining and, 91
  at entries, 72
  fostering, 53
  in small shared spaces, 96
Social space, separate, 62–63
Space, 50
  control over, 79
  between inner and outer realms, 75
  previewing, 91–92
  purposeful, 87
  shared, 94–96
  thresholds between, 61–62
  unencumbered and supportive, 81–82, 116, 128
Spatial character, 47–48
  at Corvallis Assisted Living, 121
  at Rosewood Estates, 111
Stability, maintaining, 105
Stability/predictability concept, 37
  design considerations for, 67–73
Staff, 104
  privacy of, 99–100
Staff kitchen, 97

Staff monitoring space, 18
Staff-resident ratio, 24
Staircase screen wall, 92
Stairways, 91–93
  at Corvallis Assisted Living, 130
  at Rosewood Estates, 118
Stairway seating spot, 75
Stand-alone facilities, 17–18
Steven Holl Architects, 74
Stimulation, in Assisted Living, 16
Stone facades, 48
Stress, in shared households, 10
Sullivan, Louis, 92
Sunrise Retirement Home, 66, 85
Sunrooms, 95
Supplies. *See* Modified delivery space and system

Thresholds, 61–62, 70
  at Corvallis Assisted Living, 125
  at Rosewood Estates, 114
Toilet rooms, 90, 91, 95
Traditional continuum of care, 9
Transitions, 61
  public to private, 60, 74
Transition spaces, layered, 95
Transportation, 17
Travel, difficulties of, 52

Unit entries, personalized, 43
University of Wisconsin/Milwaukee School of Architecture and Urban Planning, x, 149

Van Zandt House, 74
Vegetative states, 6
Venturi, Rauch Scott Brown, Associates, 41
Vertical disorientation, 92
Vesass, Tarjei, 35
Vessel of memory/vessel of soul concept, 36
  design considerations for, 46–49
Visitors, 66–67
  accommodating, 87
Visual connections, 87

Walking circuits, 72–73. *See also* Circulation routes
Wall plane, articulated, 58
Wandering behavior, 73. *See also* Cognitive impairment
Wayfinding, 45
  clarity in, 69
  at entry places, 71–72
Weingarten Residence, 87
Well-being, 29
  links to, 105
Wellness, xii
  "home" as critical to, 26
Wheelchair accessibility, 78, 81, 97–98
Window seats, 42, 59
Woodside Place, 21, 85, 100
Work/office space, 99–100
Wright, Frank Lloyd, 71